THE PROPHETIC MINISTRY

Ulf Ekman

Sumrall Publishing

THE PROPHETIC MINISTRY
First published in English, 1990
Third edition, 2001

ISBN 1 58568 210 1

Published by Sumrall Publishing

Acknowledgments
Unless otherwise indicated, Scripture quotations are
from the *New King James Version* of the Bible, copyright ©
1979, 1980, 1982 Thomas Nelson Publishers, Inc.

Scripture quotations noted NIV are from the *Holy Bible,
New International Version*, copyright © 1973, 1978, 1984
International Bible Society. Used by permission of Zondervan
Bible Publishers

Table of Contents

Foreword

I am convinced that we are living in the closing days of this dispensation. If any ministry is important in these climatic days it is the prophetic ministry.

I believe that God in His infinite wisdom has reached down from heaven into Uppsala, Sweden, and placed a prophetic mantle on Ulf Ekman. This young pastor leads the thriving congregation, one of Sweden's largest churches that is making an impact around the world.

Pastor Ekman has ministered at two of our World Conventions. His prophetic ministry produced life-changing results in the lives of our leadership and membership.

This book provides essential guideposts for the operation of the prophetic ministry today. Ulf Ekman reminds us that, "not everything that is labeled with the epithet 'thus saith the Lord' is automatically a prophetic message. Some of these utterances may just be good wishes. But when you are convinced that God is speaking, you need to receive and begin to act on what He says."

The primary focus of this book, and its author, is the all-important fact that the prophetic ministry receives its anointing and its purpose from Jesus, the Prophet. Jesus, seated at the right hand of the Father in heaven, gives this ministry gift to the prophet here on earth (Eph 4:11).

In reading this book you will be challenged by many questions concerning the prophetic ministry. I remember so well the prophecies I received concerning the Full Gospel Business Men's Fellowship. There were times I felt like giving up, but God had spoken through His prophets. Ulf's closing words are the testimony of my life, "God's Word is true, He longs to care for you and to guide you in His paths of His righteousness. He is eager to reveal His Word to you." So, when you listen, receive and preserve the word, you will witness the plan of God being fulfilled in your life and you, too, can testify that "What He has promised, that He has done."

Demos Shakarian

Preface

There is a tremendous need to hear clearly from God in this day and age. His prophetic Word contains clarity, beauty and strength. It pierces people's hearts and completely transforms their lives—it is God speaking His eternal Word directly from heaven.

The Word of God created the heavens and the earth, and the entire universe is held together by the power of this Word today. It is a holy Word that heals, delivers, saves and preserves men in holiness and victory. Time and time again the Bible exalts the Word that comes from heaven. It is a precious Word that expresses and reveals the ways of God.

The prophetic ministry involves the special task of listening to God and then delivering His Word to others. The prophet has a ministry of revelation and his faithfulness to the written Word is essential to seeing God's will fulfilled here on earth. The Lord will raise up thousands of servants who will be entrusted with His Word and it will be said of them, just as it was of the prophet Samuel, *the Lord was with him and let none of his words fall to the ground* (1 Sam 3:19).

God desires to entrust you with His Covenant Word so that you can hear clearly from heaven, do what He tells you to do and thus, see His will become a reality in your life.

Ulf Ekman

THE GIFT OF
PROPHECY

1

Prophesy!

But Peter, standing up with the eleven, raised his voice and said to them, "Men of Judea and all who dwell in Jerusalem, let this be known to you, and heed my words. For these are not drunk, as you suppose, since it is only the third hour of the day. But this is what was spoken by the prophet Joel: 'And it shall come to pass in the last days, says God, That I will pour out of My Spirit on all flesh; Your sons and your daughters shall prophesy, Your young men shall see visions, Your old men shall dream dreams. And on My menservants and on My maidservants I will pour out My Spirit in those days; And they shall prophesy. I will show wonders in heaven above And signs in the earth beneath: Blood and fire and vapor of smoke. The sun shall be turned into darkness, And the moon into blood, Before the coming of the great and notable day of the Lord. And it shall come to pass that whoever calls on the name of the Lord shall be saved'" (Acts 2:14-21).

The Age of the Old Covenant had just come to an end. Whenever one dispensation or age is over, the Lord always has His servants who prophesy what will take place in the coming age. Some of these servants simply prophesy during the old age about the coming one without ever seeing it. Other prophets cross back and forth between the two dispensations.

In addition to these two types of ministries, God also has those in the new dispensation who proclaim what has been prophesied during the previous one. This is the case in the above scriptures; God's servant proclaimed the prophecies given during the Old Testament that foretold the New Covenant.

God had especially, trained and prepared these people for such a commission. Peter was one of them. What he was preaching had already been prophesied by the prophet Joel, in the Old Testament. This prophesy came into being on the Day of Pentecost in the New Covenant and will continue until the return of Jesus Christ, which is the last day of the Church Age.

When we refer to the Age of the Church we are talking about the Age of the Spirit. It is the Holy Spirit who separates the Age of the Church from other ages. He has been poured out during this dispensation in a way unlike any other age in the history of the world. He has been made available to all of us and has been poured out over all flesh.

"All flesh" refers not only to each individual believer, but it also means that you will find the Holy Spirit wherever there are people. This does not mean, though, that the Holy Spirit dwells in everyone. He only dwells in those who call on the Name of the Lord and have been born again. However, in our world today, as never before, the Holy Spirit is present among people.

We Can Know the Times

We are living in the last days. They began on the Day of Pentecost. Peter lived at the start of the Age of the Church and now we are living at its conclusion. How should we be sure of this? Because just as the Holy Spirit revealed to Peter the time in which his generation was living, He will do the same for us.

Surely the Lord does nothing unless He reveals His secret to His servants the prophets (Amos 3:7). We will know when Jesus returns. "But," you say, "the Bible says that no man

12

knows the day or the hour of Jesus' return, not even the Son." That is true, but as that day approaches, then we will know.

The New Testament tells us prophetically that the Lord will soon return. It has been two thousand years since this was spoken and His return is closer now than it was back then. Obviously, what God means by "soon" is not what we mean when we use the word. We must, therefore, understand the prophetic word.

The Holy Spirit will prepare the Church so that it knows approximately when Jesus will return. Just as He spoke to His servants in the Old Testament and prepared them for what was to come, He will also prepare us. Both Anna and Simeon knew that the Messiah would come. Simeon had received a prophetic message telling him that he would not see death before he had seen the Christ (Luke 2:26).

I am convinced that God is able to say the same thing in this age; speaking just as clearly to people when the time is near: "You will not die until you have seen Jesus return."

However, we must learn to distinguish true prophecy from vain fantasy so the Holy Spirit can bring forth the genuine article and thus restore respect for the prophetic ministry and anointing. Then, all that God desires to say through His prophets can be said and the Church can be properly prepared.

The Prophetic is Being Emphasized

Let's look again at what the prophet Joel said:

And it shall come to pass in the last days, says God, that I will pour our My Spirit on all flesh; your sons and your daughters *shall prophesy,* your young men *shall see visions,* your old men *shall dream dreams.* And on My menservants and on My maidservants I will pour out My Spirit in those days: and they *shall prophesy.* I will show wonders in heaven above and signs in the earth beneath: blood and fire and vapor of smoke (Acts 2:16-19).

13

The last days began on the Day of Pentecost. We are currently living in the very last of the last days. This scripture certainly applies now. It tells us that *the first sign that the Spirit of God has been poured out is that your sons and daughters will begin to prophesy.* In this context remember what it says in First Corinthians 14:1: *desire spiritual gifts, but especially that you may prophesy.*

Your sons and daughters will prophesy. Young men will see visions and old men will dream dreams. All of this is very much a part of the prophetic anointing. *And on My menservants and on My maidservants I will pour out My Spirit in those days: And they shall prophesy.* Not until after this, does it say in verse 19: *I will show wonders in heaven above and signs in the earth beneath.*

In this portion of scripture, God makes a total of four references to prophecy or a prophetic anointing manifesting in some way. God places an emphasis on the prophetic word and the prophetic message, which is God's Word to people for the time in which they live. If we miss this Word, we will miss everything, for God will confirm His prophetic Word with signs, wonders and miracles.

The Holy Spirit will especially do these things in the days that lie ahead. There will be changes in the spiritual realm and God will begin to speak through His prophets as never before. Therefore, it is important that you understand what a prophet is, what he is not, and the difference between the prophet and the other ministry offices and how these ministries are to cooperate together. There will be great strength in churches where the ministry gifts are allowed to express themselves and operate in the way God wants them to operate.

You and I are a part of the New Covenant and we have received the Spirit of God which, enables us to prophesy, or speak words from God. The fact that all believers can be filled with the Holy Spirit and can prophesy is the mark of the New Covenant. However, there is a difference between prophesying and being a prophet. But God wants you to prophesy so that the Holy Spirit can speak through you.

There has sometimes been an overabundance of prophecies and spectacular occurrences. But this does not mean that God does not want to see the genuine article. In fact, God shows that He is enthusiastic about prophecy when, in the very first prophecy of the New Covenant, He repeatedly exhorts His servants to prophesy.

More Than Just Words

Prophecy is remarkable because it seems to be only words. No visible miracle takes place. All you can hear are words. But while one person may hear only words, another may hear God Himself speaking and completely changing his life. He brings correction where things were heading in the wrong direction and reveals what will take place in the future, sometimes in the most peculiar way.

God wants you to prophesy accurately in the Holy Spirit so your life will be like that of Samuel. In First Samuel 3, it says that none of his words fell to the ground; every one of them was fulfilled. Every single word he prophesied was inspired by the Holy Spirit and came to pass, some in remarkable ways. This is a true prophetic ministry; it is this that God desires—and that the enemy despises.

God desires tens of thousands of prophets. Before Jesus returns He will raise them up, and they will speak as they are led by the Holy Spirit. There is nothing better than hearing from heaven. It is much less confusing than listening to a sermon full of someone's personal opinions—someone who has put a few illustrations together and used a parable or two in an attempt to create the right atmosphere.

This does not interest us—we want to hear from heaven. How wonderful when the Holy Spirit comes over a servant of the Lord and you simply know: This is God speaking!

When God speaks, the foundations of the earth are shaken. When He declares something, everything is changed. When God speaks, we must listen carefully—because we have often missed the prophetic word thinking we already knew how, when and through whom He should speak.

You have no right to put conditions on God. Balaam was rebuked through a donkey for doing this (see Num 22:28). If you are open to let God speak, like Samuel, you will learn to recognize His voice. At times it can be difficult to tell if what we are hearing is God speaking or just your own imaginations. Is it revelation from heaven or is it just a pie in the sky?

Learn to Recognize the Lord's Voice

Samuel was unable to recognize the voice of God at first. He thought it was Eli, the priest, calling for him.

God woke Samuel up one night when he was between 7-10 years old, and not recognizing the voice, Samuel thought it was Eli speaking and so he got up and went to him. When he returned to his bed, God spoke to him a second time and again he ran to Eli.

By the third time, Eli understood that God must be speaking to the boy and consequently instructed him to respond to the Lord the next time. So Samuel returned to bed and when God called to him again, he replied, *Speak, for your servant hears* (1 Sam 3:10).

God brought the most serious message of a generation to this little boy. The most powerful prophetic word to be spoken for forty years came to Samuel that night. God concluded one epoch and introduced another by using a young boy no older than 10. The prophetic anointing can come at an early age!

So Samuel lay down until morning, and opened the doors of the house of the Lord. And Samuel was afraid to tell Eli the vision. Then Eli called Samuel and said, "Samuel, my son!" He answered, "Here I am." And he said, "What is the word that the Lord spoke to you? Please do not hide it from me. God do so to you, and more also, if you hide anything from me of all the things that He said to you." Then Samuel told him everything, and hid nothing from him. And he said, "It is the Lord. Let Him do what seems good to Him" (1 Sam 3:15-18).

No wonder that Samuel was afraid! God had given him a message of judgment for Eli. We may not fully appreciate what we are asking for when we ask God to make us prophets. We may well get to prophesy but, like Jeremiah, we could also end up at the bottom of a well! (Jer 38:6).

Saul Among the Prophets

There is nothing more powerful or wonderful than hearing from heaven. You can hear the voice of God in a variety of ways. Of course, you can hear Him personally, but He can also speak to you through prophets. When this happens, you need to be able to recognize and accept it as a word from heaven. The prophet is not communicating his own ideas to you; God Himself is speaking.

Although we do not all stand in the office of a prophet, every one of us can move in a prophetic anointing. If you are a part of a group where there is a strong prophetic leaning, you will come under that anointing as well. You may be in a meeting when a powerful prophetic anointing is present and find that this anointing also comes on you.

Even Saul came under a prophetic anointing and began to prophesy. He was actually searching for David in order to kill him. However, David was in Ramah with the prophet Samuel, and together they went to Naioth where there was a group of prophets and all of them began to prophesy.

While they were all prophesying, Saul was on his way there and he too began to prophesy. His intention was to kill David, and perhaps even Samuel. However, in spite of this he still came under the anointing. He prophesied and lay on the ground all day and all night and from this, came the phrase: *Is Saul also among the prophets?* (1 Sam 19:24)

In other words, you can come under a prophetic anointing simply by being in a place where this anointing is in operation. You do not need to be a prophet. Saul was not a prophet, he was a king and had another ministry altogether. But a prophetic anointing came upon him when he was among the prophets.

This account also shows us that people can come under a strong prophetic anointing without having order in their personal lives. Nothing may work for them when they come out from under that anointing. For some reason they do not retain it. The anointing does not remain in them but is only around them. However, when this anointing remains within someone and is established in his/her life, it will work in every situation.

You can flow in a powerful prophetic anointing without being a prophet; God still has His prophets. However, whether or not you are called to stand in the prophetic office, every manservant and maidservant, every young man and old man, and every son and daughter is called to prophesy—everyone shall prophesy.

An Anointing of Confrontation

The prophet, though, is equipped with supernatural anointing in different areas. He has a unique ability to confront—idol worshipers, occultists, prophets of Baal, whoever it may be—and to speak with a sharp anointing like no other ministry in order to demonstrate who is the true God.

The Bible prophesied that John the Baptist would come in the spirit and power of Elijah to turn the disobedient to the wisdom of the just. Unlike any other ministry, the prophetic ministry has the ability to break through disobedience and cause people to obey and submit to God.

The gift of prophecy has this same function:

Therefore tongues are for a sign, not to those who believe but to unbelievers; but prophesying is not for unbelievers but for those who believe. Therefore if the whole church comes together in one place, and all speak with tongues, and there come in those who are uninformed or unbelievers, will they not say that you are out of your mind? But if all prophesy, and an unbeliever or an uninformed person comes in, he is convinced by all, he is judged by all. And thus the secrets of his heart are revealed; and so, falling down on his face, he will worship God and report that God is truly among you (1 Cor 14:22-25).

Where the gift of prophecy and a prophetic anointing are present in a meeting, people are convicted of sin. This does not mean that you stand up and prophesy against them; the presence of a prophetic anointing in the room is enough.

In the spring of 1989, I visited a church for a few days. One evening the Lord told me to prophesy instead of preach. So I prophesied all evening long, for almost an hour and a quarter.

While I was prophesying, the Spirit of God reminded the pastor of the church about First Corinthians 14. He said, "What happens when the spirit of prophesy is in operation? People are convicted of sin." So as soon as I was finished, the pastor rushed up onto the stage and gave an invitation for salvation and about ten people ran forward and were saved.

God showed this pastor that a Gospel message is not always necessary before people can be saved. The spirit of prophesy itself brings conviction that causes people to submit their hearts to God.

I remember once when I was prophesying about the future. Afterwards a woman told me that while I was prophesying, the person sitting next to her began to throw away cans of chewing tobacco and cigarettes into a nearby wastepaper basket. The Spirit of God came over him and he began to sob and say aloud several times, "I have to clean up my life."

This man became convicted. He was not saved; he just sat there listening as I prophesied about the army of the Lord and the days to come. He may not have understood anything I was saying in the natural, but the prophetic anointing convicted him that God was there. As a result, he had to get rid of his sin.

Conviction of Sin

The first response to the prophetic anointing is a desire for purity. No other anointing deals with impurity in such a strong manner as the prophetic anointing. When this anointing came over Isaiah and he saw the Lord in His temple, his first reaction was: *Woe is me, for I am undone! Because I am a man of unclean lips, And I dwell in the midst of a people of unclean lips; For my eyes have seen the King, The Lord of hosts* (Isa 6:5).

The prophetic anointing creates a need for purity in people. It brings a conviction of sin and causes them to fall to their knees and say, "God is here, I need to be saved!"

This does not mean that you must prophesy and say, "The Lord is telling me that you need to be saved." Of course, there may be times when you receive such a word of knowledge, but when you prophesy or preach prophetically, a spirit of holiness and purity descends from the throne of God and convicts people of their sin. This is what makes them want to get rid of their chewing tobacco, pipes, cigarettes, syringes and whatever else they may have in order to receive Jesus.

Therefore, we should not try to "take it easy" and preach an "evangelistic" message in order not to "scare people away." That kind of thinking is wrong. The Spirit of God may indeed lead you to preach an evangelistic message, but if you soulishly make up your mind to do so, you jump out of the spirit and into the realm of the soul. The result will be either that no one is saved or that people merely make a superficial confession of Christ without the Word of God having truly penetrated their lives. They never become pure or free and never enter into the ministry that the Holy Spirit has for them.

Getting people saved is just a fraction of our ministry as Christians. These people then need instruction in the Word of God. They need to be built up in the faith so that they become fellow workers. Many are saved but they are not God's laborers.

God wants you to be a laborer who is fully equipped for every good work. This is the function of the prophetic anointing in the Church; to edify the believers and help them find the place God has for them.

THE PROPHET—
ONE OF THE FIVE
MINISTRY GIFTS

2

The Prophet From Nazareth

God, who at various times and in different ways spoke in time past to the fathers by the prophets, has in these last days spoken to us by His Son, who He has appointed heir of all things, through whom also He made the worlds (Heb 1:1-2).

There were three ministries in the Old Testament that God used when He wanted to speak His Word on earth—the king, the priest and the prophet. The entire Old Testament affirms this. The prophets were the voice and the mouthpiece of God here on earth.

Without the prophets, we would not know God's character and nature nor have any idea of His will and plans. Praise the Lord for the prophetic office! God touched people, His Spirit came upon them and they opened their mouth and prophesied, in spite of the fact that they hardly knew what they were saying at times. They simply spoke as the Holy Spirit gave them utterance.

Every one of them prophesied concerning the coming Messiah. Each book of the Old Testament is about Him and when Jesus came, He was the greatest prophet of them all—He was the Prophet with a capital "P."

For these nations which you will dispossess listened to soothsayers and diviners; but as for you, the Lord your God has not appointed such for you. The Lord your God will raise up for you a Prophet like me from your midst, from your brethren. Him you shall hear, according to all you desired of the Lord your

God in Horeb in the day of the assembly, saying, "Let me not hear again the voice of the Lord my God, nor let me see this great fire anymore, lest I die." And the Lord said to me: "What they have spoken is good. I will raise up for them a Prophet like you from among their brethren, and will put My words in His mouth, and He shall speak to them all that I command Him" (Deut 18:14-18).

This is a prophecy concerning the Prophet Himself, Jesus of Nazareth. Jesus stood in a variety of ministry offices; one of them being the ministry of the prophet.

Jesus—The Origin of the Gifts

Following Jesus' death and resurrection, two disciples were walking along the road to Emmaus. They did not understand any of the events that had just taken place. We are just the same; without revelation we understand nothing. We live our lives in a hazy mist and in a state of complete confusion. We may say things, but be unaware of what they really mean. We have no use for well-meaning words—what we need are prophetic messages!

When Jesus met these disciples and asked them what had happened, they replied, speaking about Him, *The things concerning Jesus of Nazareth, who was a Prophet mighty in deed and word before God and all the people* (Luke 24:19). They recognized Jesus as a mighty prophet. However, He was not just a prophet, He was *the* Prophet of whom the prophets had prophesied in every book of the Old Testament.

The prophetic office of the New Testament receives its calling, its anointing and its purpose from Jesus, the Prophet. The Prophet Jesus, seated at the right hand of the Father in heaven, gives this ministry gift to the prophets here on earth.

In Ephesians 4:11 the Bible gives us a list of the ministry gifts, and among them is that of the prophet. Jesus operated in all of these ministry offices. He was an apostle: *the apostle and high priest of our confession* (Heb 3:1). He was a prophet: the Prophet, and He was also an evangelist, a pastor and a teacher.

Every individual ministry gift today receives its calling and anointing from the respective aspect of the ministry of Jesus. Jesus continues to be a prophet in the Church today. He is still an apostle. He is an evangelist, pastor and teacher. He carried out each of these ministries through His body while He was here on earth, and He still does the same today through His Body, the believers.

Jesus speaks through His mouthpiece here on earth; the mouths of believers in general, and the ministry gifts in particular. He performed mighty miracles with His hands and laid them on sick people while He was here on earth. He still does this through the hands of believers today. He does the same things, in the same way today, that He did when He walked on earth.

While Jesus was here on earth He used His body, and He is still using His body, which today is the Body of Christ. The ministry gifts are a part of Jesus' earthly ministry now, and one of these gifts is the prophet.

3

The Believer's Anointing

And these signs will follow those who believe: In My name they will cast out demons; they will speak with new tongues; they will take up serpents; and if they drink anything deadly, it will by no means hurt them; they will lay hands on the sick, and they will recover (Mark 16:17-18).

All of us as believers want God to work through us. We want Him to speak through us and we desire to see signs and wonders. This longing became a part of us when we were born again.

We must understand that each believer is called by the Lord to preach the Gospel. We are also to lay our hands on the sick. When we are obedient to Jesus' instructions, an anointing from heaven will come on us. This anointing helps us to preach and it heals the sick!

Every time you hear Mark 16:17-20 you should rejoice and say, "This is for me!" Then as you act in obedience to the Holy Spirit, you will experience His anointing flowing through you, and you will see signs and wonders just as Jesus has promised.

When your mind grows tired of hearing these verses, it is usually a sign that you have allowed other things to preoccupy you and take precedence over Jesus in your life. In this case, it is necessary to rid yourself of these things and regain your love for the Lord. You need to refresh your enthusiasm concerning the things God will do in and through you.

As believers, every one of us can be powerfully used by God. However, it is important that we do not find our identity in what we do, but in who we are in God as His children. Then God can do a thorough work in our own lives before He begins to work through us. If we step into our calling too quickly, before God has had time to finish His work in us, we run the risk of falling.

We may create a great deal of difficulty by prophesying out of rejection, making things up based on self-assertion and generally being driven by insecurity. In fact, we would be following man rather than God, if we did this. Consequently, God must first do a work in our own lives to remove insecurity, fear of man and rejection so we can be whole inside and secure in Him. His anointing can then flow unhindered in our lives and we will operate powerfully in the ministry God has given us.

As a minister of the Word, you will always encounter a measure of opposition. However, if you are called to be a prophet, it is vital that you have victory over rejection. If there is one ministry, above all the others, that will encounter rejection, it is that of the prophet. You must allow God to deal with you and bring strength and victory in this area if you are to succeed.

Do not be too quick to become specialized and determine what you "are." As God leads you on into new things, you will have reason to change your mind more than once! The best attitude is to simply say, "I am a believer, I love Jesus, I love people and I do what the Holy Spirit leads me to do!" That is all you need to say. With this attitude, God can lead you step by step into whatever His unique calling is for your life.

For the Edifying of the Church

In the New Covenant, Jesus is the head of the Church, which is His Body. According to First Corinthians 12:28 He has given gifts to the Church; the ministry gifts. These gifts are designed to edify the Body of Christ.

And He Himself gave some to be apostles, some prophets, some evangelists, and some pastors and teachers, for the equipping of the saints for the work of ministry, for the edifying of the body of Christ, till we all come to the unity of the faith and the knowledge of the Son of God, to a perfect man, to the measure of the stature of the fullness of Christ; that we should no longer be children, tossed to and fro and carried about with every wind of doctrine, by the trickery of men, in the cunning craftiness of deceitful plotting (Eph 4:11-14).

These five ministry offices come from heaven as gifts to the Body of Christ. They are given directly from God, the giver of every good and perfect gift. Each of these ministries operates today. As long as Jesus is the head of the Church these gifts will exist, and it is necessary that they do.

Some people claim that believers are sufficiently edified and move so powerfully in the gifts of the Spirit that the ministry gifts are no longer needed. That is wrong! If the ministry gifts are removed and the need for them denied, the believers will be unable to grow and mature into what God wants them to be. Without this maturity we are like children who are tossed back and forth by every wind of doctrine and open to the trickery of men.

The ministry gifts are the best gift God has given to both the universal and the local body of Christ. By fulfilling their own unique task, the ministry gifts are able to guarantee that there will be the required maturity, stability, direction and strength in the Church. Then each individual member can find his or her place and do what he or she is called to do.

A church will not mature and grow powerful in God unless strong ministries of this nature exist. Why not? Because the purpose of these ministries is to give correction, encouragement, comfort, help, inspiration, exhortation, discipline and anything else that is needed to make the members of the Body of Christ mature men and women of God in Christ Jesus.

Therefore, the purpose of the devil's deception is clear when he suggests, "Pastors are not needed. The ministry gifts are no longer necessary. All believers are pastors; everyone is an evangelist!" These statements are lies!

It is true that all of us as believers have an evangelistic anointing on our lives. We also have a prophetic anointing on our lives, just as we have an apostolic, a pastoral and a teaching anointing. Every believer has an element of each of these anointings. It is a part of our equipment as believers.

It leads us to want to teach the Word of God, to take care of people, to help them move on with God, to exhort them and prophesy over them. It causes us to want to go out and personally witness and win others. However, although these areas are in us as believers, they do not automatically make us an apostle, prophet, evangelist, pastor or teacher. What we have is simply the believer's anointing—an anointing that is extremely powerful.

Be in the Right Place!

The greatest anointing and manifestation of the Spirit of God in the last days will not be that of the evangelist the apostle or the prophet; it will be the believer's anointing—sons and daughters young men and old men who prophesy. When we realize this we will have no problem with feeling inferior or rejected because we do not have a major ministry. We will no longer wonder what we should be doing.

We will know that we are anointed by God and that the Lord wants us to prophesy. This is more than just speaking out prophecies. It also involves prophetic preaching from the Word of God, followed by Jesus confirming His Word with signs, wonders and miracles. This is something we can all do, from the least to the greatest.

As you do these general things as a believer, the Lord will speak to you regarding the specific tasks He has for you. There are many different kinds of callings. Not all of them are to one of the fivefold ministries, although they are all just as much a calling from God.

You should not have your mind soulishly fixed on trying to be something special. Some people believe that a calling to the fivefold ministry is the only thing that can give them any worth. However, even if you are a car salesman who is anointed by the Holy Spirit, you are no less important than a prophet. You simply have a different function. You can be just as led by God, just as anointed and just as satisfied.

It is much better to be a satisfied car salesman than a miserable preacher, and vice versa. Many people who are called, to an evangelistic ministry perhaps, deceive themselves and begin to get involved in business in an attempt to "bring in millions for the work of God." They live the rest of their lives in misery. They should have served God and trusted Him to meet their needs rather than being so greedy for money.

In the book of Ephesians it says that Jesus gave us gifts. What should you do with a gift? If you are an ordinary educated person you would open it, look at it and express gratitude for the gift. The Bible says that every good gift and every perfect gift is from above, and comes down from the Father of lights (James 1:17).

The ministry gifts that God gives are good; He gives only diamonds, jewels and gems. These are the kinds of gifts God gives, only good gifts. When He gives such good gifts to His Bride, the Church, we need to accept them, receive them and carefully learn how the Holy Spirit flows through them.

This is how we are edified and strengthened in God. We will not become wrongly dependent on the gifts, but we will become increasingly dependent on God. Through these ministry gifts we become strong in the Lord.

4

The Fivefold Ministry Gifts

And He Himself gave some to be apostles, some prophets, some evangelists, and some pastors and teachers (Eph 4:11).

And God has appointed these in the church: first apostles, second prophets, third teachers, after that miracles, then gifts of healings, helps, administrations, varieties of tongues (1 Cor 12:28).

God is the One who Appoints

God has appointed these ministry gifts in the Church, and this guarantees that they will function properly. In many places in the Old Testament we can see what happens when men appoint ministries. A prime example is Jezebel, for instance, who appointed the 450 prophets of Baal. She served them food every day and their only task was to prophesy good concerning her.

"Mirror, mirror on the wall, who's the fairest of them all?"

"You are," her prophets would say, "because you give us food!"

She had bought them. They were dependent on her and they did not dare prophesy anything but what she wanted to hear. She pulled their strings and all 450 of them prophesied for her. They may have asked, "What's for dinner today?"

"Pork chops!" she might have said.

And their immediate response to this would have been, "Thus saith the Lord: It will go well with Jezebel!"

This is just how it was. They were completely dependent on her and they liked the arrangement. Daily they sat nibbling away at her table until one day a *true* prophet came. Then their days of nibbling were over, mainly because they no longer had heads to nibble with!

The Apostle

When the Bible says that God has appointed "first apostles," it does not mean that He has placed them up on a pedestal. Instead, it means that the apostle has been placed *at the very front*. The idea of a vertical triangle with some sort of pope seated at the top should be discarded. Imagine instead a horizontal triangle that looks like a plow. God has positioned the apostle at the tip of this plow.

The apostle can be likened to a *general practitioner*. He has the ability to operate in all of the ministry offices. The apostle can enter a town and work as an evangelist, preaching the Gospel so that people are saved. When he has done this, he becomes a pastor. He starts a church and pastors the newly-saved. While pastoring them, he gives them systematic teaching from the Word of God.

When he notices them becoming overly enthusiastic about one element of his teaching, such as spiritual warfare, he begins to prophesy over them to bring them up out of the ditch and onto the road again. At the same time, though, he reminds them to avoid the other ditch. In this way, the apostle has functioned in *all the ministries*.

The apostle is a highly qualified regional and national general practitioner. He has the ability to do a wide variety of tasks. But when he has evangelized, started a church, been a pastor, and taught and prophesied over the people, he begins to feel unsettled. It is time for him to move on. However, he does not disappear as quickly as the evangelist, who often leaves as soon as his job is completed.

There are different types of apostles. Some of them remain, but many are mobile. Paul was always on the move. He would start a church, lay its foundation and move on. His ministry was extremely foundational. *According to the grace of God which was given to me, **as a wise master builder,*** he says, *I have laid the foundation, and another builds on it. But let each one take heed how he builds on it* (1 Cor 3:10).

The Prophet

More than anything else, the prophet is *God's index finger.* His preaching is not always methodical and it can often seem somewhat unsystematic. He operates under a prophetic anointing when he preaches.

The prophet sees people's hearts and motives. He is also able to foresee future events. He points out the direction that God wants to move in and, together with the apostle, he lays the foundation of the church.

He is sharper and more precise than any of the other offices when it comes to speaking the Word of God. With his scalpel he is able to reveal the condition of the entire church. He looks beneath the surface, knowing that although things may be outwardly beautiful, there can be cancer lurking within. If the church is to survive, the tumor must be removed.

God always removes sin by its roots. This is the ministry of the prophet. He does not start by saying, "I have a little three-month project for your church. Let's just begin now to carefully discuss a few things of minor importance. We won't call it 'sin' to begin with, but rather a 'mistake', so that the people have time to get used to the idea. Then, maybe in about three months, I thought I'd talk about one or two things that are not quite right."

A prophet never talks like this. Perhaps a backslidden pastor talks this way, one whose "love" has gone *too* far.

There are evangelists who do away with the idea of hell in their desire to get people saved. But this is not the way in which people are saved, because hell is a reality. The prophet does not excuse himself for mentioning hell. Instead, he states the truth quite bluntly: "You will end up in hell if you don't repent!"

The prophet talks in black and white. Therefore it is vital, for his sake, that he is in line with God. Otherwise he may come to the operating table with an axe, which is not God's will.

The Evangelist

The evangelist reaches out farther than all the other ministers—*he reaches out to the world.* He is not at all an exhorter who travels from one church to the next preaching revival. Such an evangelist would only end up in frustration. An evangelist who is confined to such a church will often try to be a prophet. He scolds the people and tells them they are backslidden for not witnessing enough.

The evangelist has a desire to reach the masses. He does not leave "the ninety-nine" in order to reach only one. You will never hear him say, "I could have had 99 people at my meeting but I settled for just one." That is not what he writes in his newsletter, nor should he, for he is a large scale combine harvester. Thousands should be in attendance at his meetings.

The evangelist wants to get people saved. Above all, his desire is for salvation, baptism in the Spirit and signs, wonders and miracles, healings and deliverance. He has an explosive ministry that attracts people. Everyone likes to watch fireworks as they explode and light up the sky with a big bang. Everyone likes amusement parks. Of all the ministry offices, the ministry of the evangelist is the most sensational.

It is a wonderful and extremely important ministry. We need thousands of evangelists, and not all of them are to be like T.L. Osborn and Reinhard Bonnke, but some are to be more locally based. It is important to remember that evangelists are needed on every level.

The Pastor

The pastor is the opposite of the prophet. He carries a supernatural *compassion and care for the sheep*. The pastor has what Jesus had when He had compassion on the crowds. The evangelist does not have compassion on the crowds. He thinks it is wonderful to see people saved and to see them healed and testify to their healing. But then he is gone, and rightly so; he needs to move on.

If someone comes to him and asks, "Do you remember when you prayed for me? Now I have another problem," he will refer them to their pastor. This is how it should be, and this needs to be understood. It is not a weakness, it is simply a part of his ministry.

The pastor has a special kind of compassion on people and a supernatural patience with them. He is always ready to try again and to give people another chance. He hears Jesus respond to the question, *how often shall my brother sin against me, and I forgive him? ...up to seventy times seven.* This is the pastor's heart; he is willing to leave the ninety-nine to search for the one lost lamb.

The pastor has a big heart and creates a family atmosphere in the church like no one else can. This prompts the people to say, "Oh, I feel right at home!" And everything is wonderful until the prophet comes along. His sense of smell is more acute than that of the pastor. "I smell sin here," says the prophet.

"Well, I suppose there are one or two people who have a few problems, but that's the way it is in every church," explains the pastor.

But the prophet declares, "There is sin here! Backsliding! Demons!"

"Oh no," says the pastor. "There are none of those here! We cast them out a long time ago!"

The pastor suddenly becomes nervous because he has been working for years to get everything to work as it should. He is willing to defend his "sheep" and feels that the prophet should be less harsh in his judgment.

The pastor can have a tendency to whitewash over dead bones. He does not do this out of a wrong heart, but out of compassion for the sheep. It's much the same as when a mother protects and defends her children even when they knowingly manipulate her.

Another risk is that the pastor compares himself with other ministry gifts which come into the church. Because the pastor is not quite as dynamic, he can easily feel insecure when the evangelist comes along. The pastor is unable to say, "I was in Rio de Janeiro yesterday and 15,000 people were saved!"

So when the evangelist relates his accomplishments and anecdotes, the pastor may be unsure and think, "He is just exaggerating! Someone should check those figures! They might not be accurate!"

It is wrong and completely unnecessary for the pastor to feel envious like this. God does not look down on him. His ministry is of equal importance. If an evangelist was put in the place of a pastor, the church would end up in a state of complete confusion and chaos.

When the prophet comes to visit a church, the pastor gulps three times: "I wonder what will happen now," he thinks to himself. The devil is quick to say, "Don't invite him again! He is so hard!" Then one of the church members will come along and say, "That was so hard!" And they are absolutely right! Cold steel is indeed hard, but operating on a cancer tumor with bare hands is impossible. Without a razor sharp knife it just does not work.

However, in the days ahead we will see the Lord raise up many pastors with a strong prophetic anointing. This does not imply that they will be lacking in love; they will simply speak the truth so that people can be free and pure and continue with God. If you have no desire to be free and pure, you should not be in a place where deliverance and holiness are preached.

God will give a great deal of strength and boldness to pastors to enable them to lead several thousand people; not just for the sake of having large numbers, but in order to help this many move on with God.

The Teacher

The teacher is extremely important. His task is to provide the church with methodical, systematic teaching. Just as a driving school instructor teaches people how to drive a car and then leaves it up to them to do the driving, the teacher also helps believers put the Word into practice in their own personal lives.

By the time a teacher is finished, truth has been established in the believers' lives to the extent that they understand how the Word operates in their day-to-day living. This revelation will bring them freedom and victory as the Word becomes a reality in their lives.

Like the pastor, the teacher can also feel frustrated about the apparent lack of miracles in his ministry. But the teacher works on a long-term basis. He has a unique ability to take the deepest, most complicated *truths* and explain them so they become *crystal clear* to the listener.

A typical response to the teaching ministry is, "Aha, now I understand!" as light is suddenly shed on things in the Word of God which have previously been obscure or vague. People leave with a feeling of satisfaction, having received revelation—not about a lot of deep, complicated issues—but regarding practical things that enable them to live a victorious life.

The Gifts are Different

Each of these ministries is necessary. They serve to strengthen and support one another. The strength of one can compensate for the weakness of another.

However, the devil would like to turn the ministry gifts against one another by causing envy and strife among them as they point out one another's weaknesses and fall out of step with each other. Therefore, order is needed within these different offices. The apostle and the prophet know God's time schedule and are better acquainted with the proper order of things than the other ministry offices.

God has appointed the apostle and the prophet to lay the foundation in the church. Those who lay the foundation of a house have a timetable for when the rest of the work is to be done.

God's will is for the ministry gifts to operate together in the local church. There should be an apostle, or at least some form of contact with such a ministry, in every local church. There should be prophets, evangelists, pastors and teachers, all in the same church. The church which meets these requirements will be a strong church that will grow and be able to withstand demonic opposition as it moves ahead and does all that God wants it to do.

When we understand the differences in the ministerial offices, we will be able to affirm one another's gifts. We do not need to be envious or nervous, but we can let others come in and do what they have been called and equipped to do.

An engineer and a lawyer have two completely distinct tasks. A carpenter is not a sales assistant. Similarly, each of the fivefold ministries is distinct and different. You have no right to judge them or to decide that they should be different from what they are. Perhaps someone fails to perform his ministry fully, but that is another issue. This does not authorize you to try and make the pastor into a prophet, or vice versa.

You need to see the gift and thank God for it. Each gift does its part, and as they work together, the entire Body of Christ is built up. We need all the gifts. The Bible warns us not to concentrate on and, thus, begin to idolize any one of them. You do not worship the gift, you worship Jesus, the giver. First Corinthians 1:10-13 talks about this.

Wholeness Is Needed

If the church has only a prophet in leadership, they will end up just prophesying and attempting to surpass one another with hallucinatory revelations until they have gone off the rails altogether. The poor sheep will not understand what is going on, and an abundance of vain imaginations will not replace real food.

The same is true for every ministerial office. Even if your church does nothing but witness and evangelize, it will not be enough. It is good that they win people for the Lord. This is what Jesus wants, but unfortunately, it is not enough.

You also need teachers who are able to instruct the newly saved and prophets who can correct them and provide them with the strength and stability they need to develop. Otherwise, even if you get 10,000 people saved, you will end up with a huge mess on your hands. Quantity is not the only thing that matters; we need quality as well.

The task of the ministerial offices is to help believers mature so they do not behave childishly and run around everywhere getting into trouble.

The same can be said of a church where only the pastoral anointing is present. There, the congregation becomes easily introspective. They enjoy one another's company and think that everything is just fine. As a result, they fall asleep and are anesthetized by religiosity. Of course, it is peaceful—everyone is fast asleep—which means that nothing is being accomplished.

You and I have no right to make a judgment based on our emotional sentiments as to what we think a church should be or do and in which direction we feel it ought to be moving. We need to hear from heaven instead.

Variation Within the Gifts

Within each gift there are a variety of both strong and weak characteristics. Among evangelists you will find those who reach out to continents, as well as those who reach out to certain cities in a particular country, or even to particular suburbs within that city. If you are an evangelist, it is vital that you discover what type of evangelist you are and on what level you are to operate.

The same is true for the prophet. Not everyone is an earth-shattering prophet like Jeremiah. Not all prophets have been appointed over countries and nations. There are prophets who have been placed in the local church.

For example, Acts 13:1 says that there were several people who worked as teachers and prophets in the church at Antioch. Consequently, as Romans 12:6 says, it is important that you do not prophesy beyond the measure of your faith. This is exactly what causes so much instability in the church, and this is not the intention of the Spirit of God.

Prophets differ from one another, evangelists differ and teachers and apostles differ from one another within their respective ministerial offices. As we accept this fact and find our place, we will begin to see the Holy Spirit arrange a pattern, or a mosaic, in each individual church and in the Body of Christ as a whole.

Rather than arguing with one another, each person walks the path to which he has been assigned. None pushes or shoves as every member does what he is called to do. Nothing can stop such a group of people!

The apostles and the prophets are foundational ministries. They are the pioneer gifts. Unless they find their proper function, the Body of Christ will not operate smoothly in anything it does. Prophets and apostles also experience a greater degree of persecution and attack than the other ministries.

Paul is a good example of this: *And lest I should be exalted above measure by the abundance of the revelations, a thorn in the flesh was given to me, a messenger of Satan to buffet me, lest I should be exalted above measure* (2 Cor 12:7).

The Prerequisite for National Revival

A teacher may bring excellent teaching to a church and as a result, really help the people. An apostle may come and bring the same teaching. Even if he were to make the teaching simpler and more basic, he would still have greater results. This is because there is an anointing over his life that causes the things he says to have an ongoing effect. What he speaks goes on to accomplish something more. Like a shock wave, it continues to shake that particular city, region or country.

The apostle and prophet can go further than the other ministries. This is why Satan hates these ministries more than the others. If he succeeds in removing these offices, the Church will be weakened and believers will spend all their time quarrelling with one another.

On the other hand, if these ministries are allowed to emerge, the Church will enjoy heavenly order. Prophets need to stand up and prophesy those things that will take place in the coming years, so the Body of Christ can hear what the Spirit is saying to the Church. This will make the Church so strong that Satan will not have a chance against it.

Much has been said with regard to how important it is that people are saved. Some say that we need revival now. And no doubt, we will have a revival, but not until the soldiers are trained, in place and aware of their tasks. The ministry gifts bring direction to the Body of Christ. They are designed to help the Body so it can do the work—then we will see mass revival.

A few years ago, I was somewhat frustrated. "God, I want to see more miracles. I want to see greater breakthrough," I cried.

Then I heard the Lord say very powerfully, "Just do what you are supposed to do. Don't look only at signs and wonders, and eventually you will see more than enough of them."

The key to victory is to do what you are supposed to do at the present moment. If God says that you are in a period of preparation, you should not run around trying to reap a harvest.

The prophet is better acquainted with God's timetable than any other minister. He can sense whether it is harvest time, time to sow, or whether it is a time to protect what has already been sown. Of course, it is always time to reap a certain amount of harvest, but there are other times when the real harvest comes.

If God has said that a harvest is coming but that now is a time to sow, harrow, plant, tidy up the garden, pull up the weeds and prepare, then this is what you should be doing. It will bring you blessing, satisfaction and joy to know that you are doing exactly what God wants you to do. At the right time, He will take you out like an arrow from a quiver, and fire you into all that He has for you.

THE PROPHETIC WORD—GOD'S BUILDING BLOCK

5

God Builds Using the Prophetic Word

For through Him we both have access by one Spirit to the Father. Now, therefore, you are no longer strangers and foreigners, but fellow citizens with the saints and members of the household of God, having been built on the foundation of the apostles and prophets, Jesus Christ Himself being the chief cornerstone (Eph 2:18-20).

When you read, you may understand my knowledge in the mystery of Christ, which in other ages was not made known to the sons of men, as it has now been revealed by the Spirit to His holy apostles and prophets: that the Gentiles should be fellow heirs, of the same body, and partakers of His promise in Christ through the gospel, of which I became a minister according to the gift of the grace of God given to me by the effective working of His power (Eph 3:4-7).

In these scriptures, the Holy Spirit is talking about the counsels of God which were previously hidden. When the fullness of time comes, God reveals His counsels. Usually, He does not tell us everything all at once and you may have noticed this in your own life. He may say one thing to begin with and then wait some time before He says something else. This is the way God has always been.

As we consider how God speaks, we need to understand that the entire history of mankind can be divided into seven fundamental periods of time. In each of these different ages, God has had spokesmen and prophets who have spoken on His behalf. They have prophesied regarding both current and future events.

An example of this can be found in the book of Daniel where the prophet is told:

Now I have come to make you understand what will happen to your people in the latter days, for the vision refers to many days yet to come (Dan 10:14).

In other words, God told Daniel, "This prophetic message is not about today, it is for something in the future."

Prophecy not only involves various time scales, it may also concern any one of three different levels. There are prophecies that deal with developments in the world and others that deal with the universal Body of Christ or specific churches. Finally, there are personal prophecies which are aimed at particular individuals.

We usually enjoy personal prophecies the most, since they concern us—and there is nothing wrong with this. A personal prophecy is very encouraging. But prophecy involves more than just this one level. It is also a means through which God reveals His plans for a local church, a geographical area, or the Body of Christ as a whole. It can speak of future events, which will affect all of mankind.

God uses various prophets, speaking in a variety of different ways, to reveal these future events to us. Therefore we need to know whether the things spoken about are to happen immediately, or at a later time.

Believe in Prophecy!

In the book of Ezra, we read about the restoration of the temple following the Babylonian captivity:

So the elders of the Jews built, and they prospered through the prophesying of Haggai the prophet and Zechariah the son of Iddo. And they built and finished it, according to the commandment of the God of Israel, and according to the commandment of Cyrus, Darius, and Artaxerxes king of Persia. Now the temple was finished on the third day of the month of Adar, which was in the sixth year of the reign of King Darius (Ezra 6:14-15).

The builders used mortar, stones and a variety of tools to build the temple. Furthermore, these scriptures also say that they successfully completed construction because of the prophesying of two prophets. The prophetic message, brought them success in their work.

This is how God builds the Church as well. We are often limited to thinking in the natural; that we need more money, that we need to expand and so on. But without a prophetic message all this is worthless. Success comes when the Holy Spirit speaks directly to the church and says, "Build in this manner. This is the right direction! Do it in this way." Therefore it is vital that the individual church believes in prophecy.

Many churches think they can do as they wish with God's prophetic word, but this is not the attitude God wants you to have. Not everything that is labeled with the epithet "Thus saith the Lord" is automatically a prophetic message. Some of these utterances may just be good wishes. However, when you are convinced that God is speaking, you need to receive and begin to act on what He says. The church is built through the prophets.

A Distant Future

As we saw earlier, when God spoke to Daniel, He told him that the vision referred to the future. Whenever a prophetic message comes, we must discover whether it refers to an event that is close at hand or to one that is in the future.

And the vision of the evenings and mornings which was told is true; Therefore seal up the vision, for it refers to many days in the future (Dan 8:26).

53

Of this salvation the prophets have inquired and searched carefully, who prophesied of the grace that would come to you (1 Pet 1:10).

Long ago, these prophets prophesied events that would take place in the distant future. We are living in the age during which every prophecy in the Bible will be fulfilled.

We are very close to the conclusion of the Last Days, the distant future described to Daniel. It is an age in which every prophetic message in the Old and New Testaments will be literally fulfilled. All things will be summed up in Jesus Christ, the chief cornerstone.

God builds the Church on the foundational teaching of the apostles and the prophets. He does not build on their personalities but on their teaching. He then continues to build the Church, piece by piece. Finally, when everything is in place, He adds the capstone and, as described in Zechariah 4:7, this is done with great rejoicing.

The capstone will be put in place in a unique manner and afterwards the house will be complete and ready to be occupied by the owner. When He moves in, a new age has begun.

Remember those who were alive at the beginning of this current age: Peter, James, John and others. Similarly, there will be those who live at the end of this age. Just as the Holy Spirit revealed things to them, He will also reveal to us the timing of certain events; whether they be in the distant, near or immediate future.

The Body of Christ needs to be instructed by the Holy Spirit regarding the ministry and anointing of the prophet, otherwise it may reject the gifts of the apostle and the prophet. Then it will be unable to be built up to perfection, and the will of God will not be accomplished.

God's will cannot be fulfilled unless His servants are given full freedom here on earth. Everything Jesus does is done through His Body. The enemy's strategy is not to attack and despise Jesus in heaven, but to attack Jesus here on earth in the form of His Body, the Church, and His servants, individually.

Nothing is of greater importance than ensuring that the prophetic Word of God is given free reign in the hearts and lives of people, individual churches and even entire nations. The Holy Spirit is in the process of preparing for such a time right now. There are more things that must be prophesied to enable the will of God to be accomplished in this day, and the Holy Spirit is laying the groundwork for this to be completed.

We must understand and have it deeply rooted in our hearts that *God builds using the prophetic word.*

Stable Churches

God built the temple, but stones, mortar, tools and willing servants to carry sand and gravel were not His primary method. No, God used His prophets to build the temple. The entire project was successful because the prophets were free to come and encourage the people prophetically, to speak out what would come to pass, to hear from heaven and to relate exactly what should be said. Because of this, their enemies were unable to prevent construction.

When the prophets are given the freedom to move in their anointing, the enemy cannot stop what God desires to build here on earth. Consequently, the ministry of the prophet is extremely important.

We are not saying that the prophet is more important than any other ministry. We are simply emphasizing this subject here. God places equal value on all the ministerial offices, but the Holy Spirit desires to place a special emphasis on the prophetic ministry at present, to prepare us for what He is about to do.

We will see apostles and prophets emerge during the nineties like never before. Indeed, we will see all of the ministry gifts in operation. However, there is likely to be more opposition against these two offices because of their foundational nature. Unless they are able to lay the foundation, the entire house will be unstable.

We know all too well that there are churches, both old and new, which are so fragile that the slightest gust of wind would blow them down.

God wants to raise up new churches. This is the desire of His heart. His Spirit is speaking of new churches, new works, and new projects throughout our country and the rest of the world. However, these new churches must be built on the foundation of the apostles and prophets with Jesus Himself as the chief cornerstone.

Of course, this does not imply that we are looking for some sort of overseers or popes. It simply means that God is releasing the ministry gifts so we can see them in proper operation.

God always does things thoroughly, since He sees the inevitable and violent storms that await us. If the foundation of a church has been thoroughly established and if the ministry gifts have had the freedom to play their part, then no demon in hell will be able to stop it. We will witness many such churches in the future.

Broadened Perspectives

We are going to see prophetic churches full of great numbers of prophets, all of whom come into the spirit and begin to prophesy. The Old Testament talks about the school of the prophets, although I do not believe this is a present-day model. The place for the school of the prophets in the New Testament is the church. Acts 13:1 says that there were prophets and teachers in the church at Antioch.

We need churches today like that of Antioch, where the ministries worked alongside one another. From this church, Paul made his journeys which turned the world upside down! He would then return to Antioch to report what had happened, to be encouraged and to gather strength for his next trip.

Similarly, *God wants every ministry to be based in a local church*. However, there have been problems in this area, not as a result of difficulties in the ministries themselves, but because of the lack of good quality local churches. If the church is so small and narrow-minded that not even a pastor is given room, the other ministry gifts are hardly likely to have the space they need either. In such a case, it is no wonder that ministers remain outside the church.

Fortunately, however, there is a great deal of positive change underway—changes in people's attitudes and thoughts. We are receiving new things and ascending to higher levels, while not merely rejecting all that we have previously experienced. The higher the level we attain in this way, the farther we will be able to see as a church. We will see things we have never been able to see before.

God will exalt the Church so that it operates as it should. However, we cannot be lifted any higher, if we are not pure and separated unto God. But if we are separated to God and spend more time thinking about Jesus than ourselves, no longer being introspective but instead sensitive to what God is doing in His Body, then He can lift us up and give us a far wider perspective.

By coming up higher, we will ascend above the clouds to a position from which we have a much better view. The same thing happens when the Word of God comes to you. Then you see more clearly than ever before, you see what the Holy Spirit wants you to do.

Vision or Passion?

It is not enough to be passionate about something; you must also have a vision that channels that passion. For example, you may have a strong desire to see people saved, but this does not necessarily make you a missionary.

Many people embark on missionary journeys and there is certainly nothing wrong with this. However, after returning from their first trip their sole reaction is to say, "Hallelujah, that was wonderful, but it sure is nice to be back home again!"

Clearly, these people were not called to travel; they simply had a passion. It is best that they spend most of their time at home where they can pray, evangelize, support and pray for those who are called to be missionaries.

Many people have a longing within that they wrongly assume to be a directive from heaven, telling them to immediately go to the mission field. It is absolutely necessary to know the difference between a general longing and desire to serve God, and a real directive from heaven. So lay aside any preconceived notions and ideas you have about your life and let the Holy Spirit speak to you.

If you have started a project that has turned out to be a failure, then set it aside! Some people are terrified of losing face should it become obvious that one of their projects was not at all from God. They feel embarrassed. But trying to flog life into a dead horse is much less enjoyable.

It is best to declare the horse dead! There is nothing wrong with doing this and God does not condemn you for it, He just wants you to walk in the truth. People will still love you and have confidence in you, regardless. If not, then it is doubtful that they had any love for you to begin with. Just be sure that what you do is from heaven.

Until now we have been enjoying a period of grace, but the further we go into this new millennium, the more shaking there will be.

If you stubbornly continue to do what has not been born of God, you will wear yourself out and bring confusion to both yourself and those around you. Then, you will find yourself sitting there with a mess on your hands, feeling thoroughly miserable and disappointed. It would be better for you to humble yourself now, come up higher in the spirit, and enjoy life to the full.

6

The Precious Word

Of this salvation the prophets have inquired and searched dili-gently, who prophesied of the grace that would come to you, searching what, or what manner of time, the Spirit of Christ who was in them was indicating when He testified beforehand of the sufferings of Christ and the glories that would follow (1 Pet 1:10-11).

This verse says that the prophets diligently searched the scriptures and gave heed to prophecy. A prophet is extremely thorough with the Word of God. When he has received a word from heaven, just as Mary treasured the word regarding Jesus, he too treasures it within himself, testing it, tasting it, examining it and looking at it. He meditates on the word he has received and keeps it within his heart.

No minister of the fivefold gifts is more at one with the message he brings, than the prophet.

He is often hesitant, as the message he delivers can be radical. The word of the Lord in the mouth of the prophet cuts and divides soul and spirit. Therefore, he is especially careful to try it and test it.

You need to have the same great appreciation for the Word of God as the prophet. God wants to give this to you so that His Word will not merely go in one ear and out the other. Every word will become precious to you.

I will stand my watch, And set myself on the rampart, And watch to see what He will say to me, And what I will answer when I am corrected. Then the Lord answered me and said: "Write the vision And make it plain on tablets, That he may run who reads it. For the vision is yet for an appointed time; But at the end it will speak, and it will not lie. Though it tarries, wait for it; Because it will surely come, It will not tarry (Hab 2:1-3).

The prophet has an extremely strong desire for the Word of God. He waits and watches for a word from the Lord, often unable to do much else until he has received it. He may be able to witness and evangelize a bit and perhaps do a little teaching, but this has more to do with his general calling and anointing as a believer, than with his prophetic ministry.

If the prophet is to operate in his true calling and anointing, he must have a word from heaven. He may become irritable, frustrated and incapable of preaching if this word fails to come. He may wait a long time, but when the word finally comes to his spirit, it is worth much more than gold to him.

It is difficult to explain the contentment and joy that a prophet feels when he hears a word from heaven, and the purpose and satisfaction he receives from it. He is not interested in taking a vacation and "relaxing." His vacation is a word from God!

Words with Results

No one should ever fabricate a prophecy but must always wait until God speaks. When He does speak to you, His word will settle in your spirit and when you later speak it out, everyone will know it comes from heaven.

God wants to mature us so that we see the end of so-called "prophecies" that are nothing more than a friendly greeting, a pat on the back, or merely a way of wishing someone well. "Thus saith the Lord, 'You're going to be just fine.' " This may indeed be what you want for that person, but it is easy enough to say the same thing without putting a "Thus saith the Lord" in front of it.

Simply say, "I am sure everything will be just fine. I bless you. Here is a good scripture for you. Receive this word." You can still encourage them without having to say, "Thus saith the Lord."

As a believer, there is a prophetic anointing which you do not have that belongs only to the prophet. However, all believers can prophesy. There is a distinction between the encouragement and exhortation by the believer on the one hand, and a prophetic anointing upon the prophet on the other. If every believer was able to prophesy from the prophet's anointing, God would have no need for prophets.

There is a great difference between the prophesying of an ordinary believer and that of the prophet. The believer prophesies edification, exhortation and comfort in the Holy Spirit, in accordance with the gift of prophecy. People are built up as a result. It is a wonderful gift and it produces a blessing.

However, when a prophet prophesies, something takes place in the realm of the spirit. A prophet can come into a church and need only prophesy a few words. Suddenly, there is breakthrough in an area that the church has struggled with unsuccessfully, for years. Bang! The breakthrough has come!

All of us can prophesy and all of us have the spirit of prophecy over us. But when a prophet says something in his capacity as a prophet, God is doing the talking. This is why he must be sure that what he says is indeed God.

It is wonderful to teach people under a teaching anointing. But when the prophetic anointing comes, it lifts people out into the spirit. What is spoken can change thousands of lives and all because of a single word from heaven!

Kenneth Hagin is a good example of this. He is a prophet. God spoke only a few words to him: "Go and teach my people faith." Today, however, millions of people's lives have been changed as a result of that prophetic message. Why? Because he took time to listen to God and find out what He was saying.

Contempt for Prophecy

One of the reasons prophets have not been released in the way God desires is because the people of God have despised prophecy. If people despise prophecy, God will simply neglect to speak to them. He will not speak to those who have no respect for prophecy and for those who prophesy.

What makes people despise and scorn prophetic things? Let's look at Eli as an example. He had two sons who engaged in fornication in the temple, who took the meat offerings before they were fully cooked and who violated the offerings of other people. This, the Bible says, produced contempt among the children of Israel and they no longer wanted to present offerings at the temple.

Eli was in total compromise in certain areas of his life. Although God had spoken to him, he did nothing about it. God continued speaking to Eli, but still he made no change. Finally, God no longer spoke to him. His sons lived depraved lives. Even though they were ministers under Eli, they lived as heathens. They brought the secular into the sacred and disgraced the temple. As a result, the people began to despise the priesthood and avoid the temple ceremonies.

If we prophesy based on our own ideas, ambitions and selfish desires, or if we prophesy only what the people want to hear, we profane what is sacred. Then, people will develop contempt for prophecy and the prophetic ministry will be unable to come into its fullness. Therefore, like the prophet Habakkuk, we must learn to wait until we have really heard from heaven.

God Speaks to the Church

A lion has roared! Who will not fear? The Lord God has spoken! Who can but prophesy? (Amos 3:8).

You cannot help but prophesy when God speaks, if you are sensitive to the Holy Spirit. You will not find yourself standing there wondering what to say or what to prophesy. No, when the Lord speaks, who can but prophesy?

Surely the Lord God does nothing, Unless He reveals His secret to His servants the prophets (Amos 3:7).

God has bound Himself to speak to the Church. He has determined to use the ministry of the prophet as His unique mouthpiece. He speaks with the prophet in detail regarding what He wishes to say to His Body.

Abraham, it says in James 2:23, was the friend of God. The Bible also says that Abraham was a prophet (Gen 20:7). Therefore, when He was planning to destroy Sodom and Gomorrah, God said, *Shall I hide from Abraham what I am doing, since Abraham shall surely become a great and mighty nation, and all the nations of the earth shall be blessed in him?* (Gen 18:17-18)

God looks at us, as individual believers and as a church, and says, "I do nothing without first speaking to you. I want to talk with you. I desire to tell you what is on my heart. I want to reveal to you my plans, and I will not let them be fulfilled until I have conferred with you."

When God then reveals His plans for His servants, the prophets, and they in turn prophesy them out, no demon, no principality, not the devil himself can hinder the prophetic word, as it flows from the mouth of the prophet.

That word will continue to have effect until God has confirmed it down to the letter. *Heaven and earth will pass away, but My words will by no means pass away* (Matt 24:35).

As you begin to understand this, you will become sincerely thankful for every prophecy you have ever received from God.

THE
NEW COVENANT
PROPHET

7

The Prophet—God's Mouthpiece

When you read, you may understand my knowledge in the mystery of Christ, which in other ages was not made known to the sons of men, as it has now been revealed by the Spirit to His holy apostles and prophets (Eph 3:4-5).

Some people claim that the prophet plays only a minor role in the New Testament. "He had a significant position in the Old Testament, but now that other ministries have been raised up, the prophet is not really needed anymore" they say. This kind of thinking is wrong.

The fact that the New Testament does not talk that much about the prophet is probably because there was already so much about him in the Old Testament. The prophetic ministry was already recognized and needed little further definition. As we know, the prophet was already in operation in Israel.

In the New Covenant, however, the situation is completely different. We are now God's Israel, the true Israel, which no longer involves only one nation, but encompasses the believers in every nation. The Great Commission has been given and Jesus has said, *Go into all the world and preach the gospel* (Mark 16:15).

At the same time, God introduced a ministry which was no longer limited just to Jerusalem and the surrounding areas, but which, went out into all the world. He introduced the ministry of the apostle. The apostle is like a traveling power station. As he travels, he continues to receive revelation. His ministry is extremely flexible. He can live in prison or preach for the emperor; he may find himself in almost every kind of situation.

However, just the arrival of the apostle does not mean that the prophet's ministry becomes obsolete. Instead, we can see that the prophets in the New Testament are extremely significant.

The revelation that Jesus is the Messiah, the Son of God, and that the Gospel is the power of God to salvation, is the foundation of the New Covenant. It was delivered by inspiration of the apostles and prophets. This alone reveals to us the importance of the prophet.

Due to our previous lack of knowledge of the prophetic ministry, God has been unable to accomplish the powerful works He desired to do in the Church. It is high time that God's will be done correctly and with dignity, led by the Holy Spirit and avoiding the many strange extremes that only cause people to feel aversion.

Separated unto God

As we consider the prophetic ministry in more detail we need to know that the first thing that the prophet possesses is *insight into the counsels of God.* The prophet has a unique gift of insight from the Holy Spirit into God's plans and purposes as well as an understanding of His timing.

Of this salvation the prophets have inquired and searched carefully, who prophesied of the grace that would come to you, searching what, or what manner of time, the Spirit of Christ who was in them was indicating when He testified before hand of the sufferings of Christ and the glories that would follow (1 Pet 1:10-11).

Amos 3:7 says that the Lord does nothing without first revealing it to His servants, the prophets. God has made an agreement with His prophets in giving them the right to speak His Word. *Behold, I have put My words in your mouth* (Jer 1:9), God told Jeremiah. Thus, Jeremiah was the mouth of God here on earth. This is exactly what the prophet is—He is *God's mouthpiece*.

There is something about the prophet that makes him withdraw from other people. He is unlike the pastor, who has a quality that makes him seek out others. Similarly, there is something in the evangelist that makes him throw himself over people. He is extremely people-oriented; it is simply a part of his calling and anointing.

However, the prophet almost withdraws from contact with others because there is something in his calling that says he must seek God, must hear His voice and must fellowship with Him.

A prophet will become frustrated if he is forced to be with people all the time or if his time is taken up with petty trifles. He needs space and a protective covering; a nest in which he can be at peace with God and hear from Him. Then suddenly, he is fired like a canon ball from a canon as he delivers the message given to him by the Holy Spirit.

This, however, does not give the prophet the right to say, "Oh, how wonderful! That's just what I wanted to hear. Now hopefully people will quit disturbing me. I think I will pull out the telephone jack and isolate myself." No, we will deal with the prophet's weaknesses in a further chapter. Nevertheless, the prophet must hear from God.

The prophet receives great opposition, and so God has given him a few extra blessings that enable him to withstand this resistance. For this reason, the Lord reveals His plans to His servants the prophets. He speaks to them, fellowships with them and informs them of His plans.

God reveals His thoughts and plans to this ministry alone. However, this happens only when the prophet fellowships with God, not when he just sits at home gorging himself on television programs! Perhaps no other ministry must be so careful in daily life. The prophet must live in purity on every level. If he fellowships with God and seeks Him first in everything, God will then reveal things to him in a very special way.

The Church is Built on Revelation

The Church is built on revelation from God. When Peter, inspired by the Holy Spirit said, *You are the Christ, the Son of the living God,* Jesus answered:

Blessed are you, Simon Bar-Jonah, for flesh and blood has not revealed this to you, but My Father who is in heaven. And I also say to you that you are Peter, and on this rock (referring to the revelation, and not to Peter) *I will build My church, and the gates of Hades shall not prevail against it* (Matt 16:16-18).

This revelation has been given by Jesus to the apostles and the prophets who have then proclaimed it under the inspiration of the Holy Spirit. The Church is built on this revelation from the Word of God, not on something strange, apart from God's Word. When a church is built on true revelation, the gates of hell cannot prevail against it.

This is the reason Satan does not like prophets. Of course, we are talking about true prophets; not self-assumed, strangely peculiar ministers, but the kind of prophetic ministry described in the Bible.

When God planned to destroy Sodom and Gomorrah, He first conferred with Abraham, saying, *Shall I hide from Abraham what I am doing?* Abraham had a special relationship with God and this same relationship applies generally to all believers today. God speaks to every believer, not just to a select few.

We are living under the New Covenant, not in the Old Covenant. God speaks to each believer, but the way He does it may vary. At times He speaks through His apostles and prophets. However, the Holy Spirit, or the Spirit of revelation, dwells in all believers. The gifts of revelation operate in every believer and not just in ministers.

It is vital that we understand this because we do not want a small, exclusive clique of prophets who sit on pedestals and exalt themselves above everyone else. Instead, we need people who are servants to the rest of the Body of Christ.

God gives revelation to His prophets by speaking to them and informing them about the future. He has no desire to conceal what He plans to do. This is wonderful! Right in the midst of this chaotic world full of cold, apathetic people, who have no idea of the things to come—what will happen on the stock market, whether there will be war, the state of the economy in general, etc.—God has appointed prophets in the Church who have something to say about each of these things.

God has something to say about every area of life.

Consider the prophet Agabus in Acts 11:28: When the Spirit of God came on him, he prophesied of a coming famine. This led the whole church to respond by storing up food and they were prepared when the famine finally came on the Roman Empire. God's special protection was over them because He had spoken through one of His prophets.

Total Identification

The prophet is God's unique mouthpiece and so, it is necessary for the Holy Spirit to purge him of anything that is not from God. The things of God must be separated from the things of the devil. Then we will avoid a lot of soulish rubbish that spreads uncertainty and confusion and only serves to produce contempt for the prophetic ministry. This separation applies to both the prophet's message and to his lifestyle.

Probably no other minister is so identified with his message as the prophet. John the Baptist said, *I am the voice of one crying in the wilderness* (John 1:23). Notice that he did not say, "I am a servant of the Lord and I usually speak on His behalf." Instead, he said *I am the voice...* He identified completely with his message and with the One who had sent him.

Therefore, it is not enough just to have the message in order; the prophet must also keep his life in order. As ministers, we are ambassadors and living epistles sent from God. Our lives are open books. We must ask ourselves: "What do people read when they look at my life?" This applies not only to our prophesying, but to the whole of our lives. What do people "read" when they look at you?

In the book of Revelation we can see an apostle operating in a prophetic ministry. The servant of the Lord may stand in several ministerial offices. Here we see John the apostle, who holds perhaps the most significant prophetic ministry in the New Testament. He prophesies all that will take place up to the return of Jesus. It is an unequaled prophesy:

I, John, both your brother and companion in tribulation, and in the kingdom and patience of Jesus Christ, was on the island that is called Patmos for the word of God and for the testimony of Jesus Christ. I was in the Spirit on the Lord's Day, and I heard behind me a loud voice, as of a trumpet, saying, "I am the Alpha and the Omega, the First and the Last," and, "What you see, write in a book and send it to the seven churches which are in Asia: to Ephesus, to Smyrna, to Pergamos, to Thyatira, to Sardis, to Philadelphia, and to Laodicea." Write the things which you have seen, and the things which are, and the things which will take place after this (Rev 1:9-11,19).

The Lord's prophets are often despised, rejected and stubbornly resisted. However, if they are true prophets, they do not mind how they are treated. They tried getting rid of John by putting him in exile on an island, and he returned with the entire book of Revelation.

The devil had thought, "Now we will get rid of this man who has caused so many problems in Asia Minor and in all the other places he has been." John had been a tremendous challenge, stirring up things the devil wanted to keep quiet and hidden. Even today preachers like John exist—ones who cause problems for the devil wherever they go. However, it is good that problems finally come to the surface so they can be dealt with and solved in the Holy Spirit.

The devil's plan was to get rid of the troublemaker, John, by confining him to the Isle of Patmos. There it was hoped that he would die in some God-forsaken grotto without the possibility of affecting the political state of affairs. He was away from Ephesus and Corinth, away from Athens, away from Jerusalem and Alexandria; he was not to be found in any of the large, significant cities of that day. He was unable to exercise any political influence, or so they thought.

But there on Patmos, on the Lord's Day, on Sunday or resurrection day, John came into the Spirit. He was confined to prison, which is not exactly considered a holy place, but on the other hand, there is no such thing as a holy place anymore. Nevertheless, the Holy Spirit came upon John in a prison and he came into the Spirit.

He did not enter a state of ecstasy as imagined by the world or described in the newspaper headlines: "Tongue-talkers go crazy! They climb the walls. Ambulances are summoned. Hysterical people scream and pull out their hair while frothing at the mouth." This is often the image, in the world's eyes, of being in the Spirit.

However, "to come into the Spirit" means that the inner man is made alert and his eyes are opened for a certain length of time. We may not see anything with our physical eyes, we may only see in the spirit. Or we may see with both our physical and our spiritual eyes. We may also have a dream or another kind of revelation.

God wants to give these things to all of His servants and children—and especially to His prophets. This is "coming into the Spirit." It is not necessarily lying and shaking under the power of God.

After these things I looked, and behold, a door standing open in heaven. And the first voice which I heard was like a trumpet speaking with me, saying, "Come up here, and I will show you things which must take place after this." Immediately I was in the Spirit; and behold, a throne set in heaven, and One sat on the throne (Rev 4:1-2).

This describes the prophet in operation. God has always spoken to them in a number of ways as they came into the Spirit.

Conversation with God

An example of this can be seen in the book of Numbers, where in a negative situation, God revealed some of the ways He speaks to His prophets.

There were two distinct types of rebellion among the children of Israel in the wilderness. One was when secondary leadership rebelled against primary leadership, and the other was when, for example, the people, with certain self-appointed leaders, rebelled against Moses.

Let's look at an instance when two of the leaders, Aaron and Miriam, set themselves against Moses. It all began with a little gossip. Some of the greatest tragedies in this world start with gossip. Remember this, and keep your mouth shut if you have nothing worthwhile to say. Padlock your lips and only open them when God gives you the key. Then you can prophesy instead.

Miriam was leprous for seven days because she joined Aaron in speaking evil of Moses because of his Ethiopian wife. To them it was unorthodox for Moses to have a non-Israelite wife.

Then Miriam and Aaron spoke against Moses because of the Ethiopian woman who he had married; for he had married an Ethiopian woman. And they said, "Has the Lord indeed spoken only through Moses? Has he not spoken through us also?" And the Lord heard it. (Now the man Moses was very humble, more than all men who were on the face of the earth.) Suddenly the Lord said to Moses, Aaron, and Miriam, "Come out, you three, to the tabernacle of meeting!" So the three came out. Then the Lord came down in the pillar of cloud and stood in the door of the tabernacle, and called Aaron and Miriam. And they both went forward. Then He said, "Hear now My words: If there is a prophet among you, I, the Lord, make Myself known to him in a vision; I speak to him in a dream. Not so with My servant Moses; He is faithful in all My house. I speak with him face to face, Even plainly, and not in dark sayings; And he sees the form of the Lord. Why then were you not afraid to speak against My servant Moses?" (Num 12:1-8).

Moses had never claimed to be the only one to whom God would speak. Miriam's statement that they too could hear from God was true, but it was said in the wrong spirit. Something which is fundamentally true, but which is said in a wrong spirit, can be fatal.

We see though, from these scripture that the natural and most common way that the prophet receives revelation from God, is through dreams and visions. For this reason the prophet is called a seer, or one who sees. The Bible says that when the Spirit of God came on Balaak, his eyes (his spiritual eyes) were opened so that he could see. This faculty is unique to the prophet—his ability to *see*. He sees the Word of the Lord as God speaks to him in pictures, dreams and symbols.

God speaks through inspiration, but *always on the foundation of the written Word* and never beyond its boundaries. What He says is always in line with His written Word.

Revelation is an atmosphere in which the prophet lives. He needs to be left in peace so he can hear from God. The worst thing to do to a prophet is to continuously tug and pull at him in an attempt to involve him in practical things that are of no concern to him. This will merely disturb him and is, in fact, often a tactic used by Satan to do just this.

The prophet needs seclusion to receive revelation and to hear, see and have dreams and visions. This is the way in which God usually reveals Himself to His prophets, but Moses was slightly different. "I speak with him face to face," the Lord said of Moses. In other words, they sat down and had a conversation.

This is also evident in the book of Jeremiah: *"The prophet who has a dream, let him tell a dream; And he who has My word, let him speak My word faithfully. What is the chaff to the wheat?" says the Lord* (Jer 23:28).

It is good when a prophet receives dreams and visions, but it is even better when he receives the Word just as it comes. Although we are speaking specifically about the prophet here, this is not something that only a few, select people throughout history have been allowed to witness, it is available to all of God's people.

The Supernatural Can Become Natural

Samuel was raised up as a prophet before the Lord during a period of decline in Israel. What sort of decline was it? First Samuel 3:1 says: *Then the boy Samuel ministered to the Lord before Eli. And the word of the Lord was rare in those days; there was no widespread revelation.*

Prophetic visions were uncommon during that period. However, God wants them to be a common occurrence. Unfortunately, they are sometimes rare among us. If we suddenly have a dream, a vision, a revelation or an angelic visitation, we are completely taken aback. Then we spend the next thirty years talking about the angel we saw, rather than relating what he actually said.

It is the equivalent of saying, "A mailman came to our house yesterday. He came to me. He was wearing a blue uniform. It was tremendous!" But the mailman is not important—what he brought is.

When we live in a prophetic climate where dreams, visions, and revelations are commonplace, there will be no room for showing off about our spiritual experiences. God is often forced to withdraw His Spirit and conceal Himself when we are unable to correctly manage His gifts.

This is why God wants the gifts of the Spirit to be in frequent use—so we do not fall off our perches just because we happen to receive a word of knowledge. It is obviously wonderful to receive such a word, but it is certainly nothing to get puffed up about. God wants every one of us to receive an abundance of words of knowledge.

God also wants prophetic visions to be common occurrences. Then it will be much easier to judge which ones really are from God and which ones are merely soulish fantasies. Prophecy does not make a person more important. The Bible warns us about becoming puffed up over angelic visitations and revelations.

Let no one defraud you of your reward, taking delight in false humility and worship of angels, intruding into those things which he had not seen, vainly puffed up by his fleshly mind (Col 2:18).

If we frequently experience dreams and visions, we will not become puffed up. We will be like Isaiah, Jeremiah and the rest of the prophets—we prophesy and then return home to our families to eat dinner. God wants you to live in a supernaturally natural way, so that living in revelation is a supernatural operation of the Church.

8

The Forerunner of a New Dispensation

Another characteristic of the prophet's ministry is the way God uses him to prepare for the next phase or stage of development in His purposes. As we have seen, the prophet has insight into the counsels of God and receives a revelation of God's intentions. In addition, God also uses him as an instrument to carry out these plans. The prophet is often a *forerunner* of what is to come.

Noah, who had a prophetic ministry, is an example of this. He prophesied God's judgment. Some people seem to think that all prophets are prophets of doom, but this is not the case. However, Noah was a prophetic sign; he lived at the end of one age and continued into the next.

The Bible reveals seven different ages throughout history: (1) The age of innocence, from creation to the Fall; (2) The age of conscience; (3) The period of human government; (4) The period of promise, the time of Abraham; (5) The period of the law, the time of Moses; (6) The age of grace, the age of the Church and (7) The millennium. Following this is eternity.

During each of these seven time periods, God deals differently with mankind. He is still the same God, but He simply administrates the course of events and manifests Himself in slightly different ways in each of the various ages. He goes from glory to glory, from one age to the next.

For example, the age of the Church is more glorious than the period of the law, just as there was greater glory during the period of the law than there was during the age of the promise. Similarly, there was more glory during the age of promise than during the period of human government, and so on.

During the first period, prior to the Fall of man, there was obviously a great amount of glory. But there will be an even greater measure of glory in eternity. We go from glory to glory.

In these God-ordained time periods, God uses His servants, the prophets, to speak out and then administrate what is to come. They are forerunners and their task is to prepare.

The Ministry of Elijah

God, who at various times and in different ways spoke in time past to the fathers by the prophets, has in these last days spoken to us by His Son, whom He has appointed heir of all things, through whom also He made the worlds (Heb 1:1-2).

When a new age was on the way—when Jesus was about to come to the earth—God sent a forerunner to prepare for His arrival. His name was John the Baptist, a very unique prophet. His one and only task was to be Elijah, since God had promised that Elijah would come once again:

Behold, I will send you Elijah the prophet, Before the coming of the great and dreadful day of the Lord. And he will turn the hearts of the fathers to the children, And the hearts of the children to their fathers, Lest I come and strike the earth with a curse (Mal 4:5-6).

These are the last verses of the Old Testament. After they were recorded, they hung in the air for a few hundred years before finally being fulfilled by John the Baptist.

The prophet can prophesy out to the world but he mainly prophesies inwardly, that is, to the Body of Christ, to prepare it for the next event in God's plan. In its deepest sense, it is a part of the preparation for the Second Coming of Jesus Christ.

We are usually under the assumption that Jesus could return at any minute since He said that He is coming soon. He is indeed coming at an hour when we do not expect Him (Matt 24:44). However, it is an hour when the *world* does not expect Him. *He cannot come at any moment.*

A wedding involves careful planning. The groom cannot say to the bride, "Shall we get married tomorrow instead?" This is not the way it is done. If it were, it would be both careless and inconsiderate. Instead, a wedding involves careful planning and preparation since it only happens once in a lifetime and is indeed one of life's greatest experiences. It may not take years of preparation, but it takes more than just one day.

It is the same for Jesus when He is to get married. He does not ask His Father, "Can't we have the wedding today?" Nor does the Father say to Jesus, "What do you think, shall we do it today?" And then He looks down to earth to see the bride full of worldliness, completely confused and not knowing which way to turn.

Do you think Jesus wants to come for such a bride? No, He will return when His bride is complete, prepared and adorned with everything in place: her crown where it should be, her diamonds correctly positioned, and surrounded by a spirit of delight and purity. Everything is ready. *Then* Jesus will come.

The work of the apostles and prophets, and especially the prophet, is to prepare the Bride of Christ. This is not always an easy task. The Bride is not always willing to be prepared. She is under a great deal of pressure to live in a way other than that which Jesus expects of His betrothed.

The task of the prophet, however, is to prepare her for the next step in spiritual development.

Repentant Hearts

When something extremely special was about to take place, when the Son of God was to come into the world, God sent a prophet whom He had promised would come—John the Baptist. The same ministry and spirit that was on Elijah was also on him.

Elijah had a unique ability to bring the people to the point of decision. Would they follow God? He asked them, *"How long will you falter between two opinions? If the Lord is God, follow him; but if Baal, follow him."* But the people answered him not a word (1 Kings 18:21).

No one said a word. They all stood quietly mumbling to themselves until fire fell from heaven. Then all at once, the people said, *The Lord, He is God! The Lord, He is God!* (1 Kings 18:39). They had made up their minds in an instant. Their hearts were immediately changed. Even the disobedient became obedient when they saw the fire come from heaven.

Part of the prophet's ministry is to turn people's minds in this way, so that the hearts of the fathers, with their backsliding and compromise, and the hearts of the sons and daughters, with their rebellion and worldliness, are once again turned to one another and, in particular, to God.

This was why the ministry of Elijah had to return. The Lord cannot come, either in His first arrival or in His final return, to anything other than a well-prepared people. It is impossible for Jesus to return, unless His Bride is ready. The task of the prophetic ministry is to prepare her.

In those days John the Baptist came preaching in the wilderness of Judea, and saying, "Repent, for the kingdom of heaven is at hand!" For this is he who was spoken of by the prophet Isaiah, saying: "The voice of one crying in the wilderness: 'Prepare the way of the Lord, Make His paths straight'" (Matt 3:1-3).

This was not only John the Baptist's task, but that of Elijah as well. Every prophetic anointing and prophetic spirit, particularly in the last days, has this function.

John the Baptist lived during the period of transition into the New Covenant. The Spirit of God was on him to prepare the way for Jesus' coming. Likewise, we who live at the conclusion of this age, must be prepared for Jesus' second coming. During these days, the same spirit that was on John the Baptist will come over not just one individual, but over the whole Church. Jesus' return will be one of the most significant events in the history of the universe and it must be prepared for thoroughly.

What exactly was the function of the prophet in the transition between the Old and New Covenants? He performed no signs or wonders. They said of John the Baptist: *John performed no sign, but all the things that John spoke about this Man were true* (John 10:41). John the Baptist's strength did not lie in signs and wonders. He himself was a sign and a wonder right from the time he kicked in the womb of his mother, Elizabeth, when she met Mary.

John the Baptist's arrival was a miracle. He was a sermon in himself. He was a living miracle. His strength lay in his ability to cause people to repent, to prepare them and to point to the Messiah. This was his ministry.

No matter what our calling is, we must only do what we have been called to do. When someone else has a calling and does something that looks more impressive, our reaction should be like that of John the Baptist, when he was told what Jesus was doing: *He must increase, but I must decrease* (John 3:30). He knew exactly what he was to do. His task, and it is a general task of all prophets, was to prepare the people and to clear the way for the Lord.

Read what the angel said to Zacharias, regarding John:

And you will have joy and gladness, and many will rejoice at his birth. For he will be great in the sight of the Lord, and shall drink neither wine nor strong drink. He will also be filled with the Holy Spirit, even from his mother's womb (Luke 1:14-15).

Do Not Flirt With the World

Every ministry requires separation. The word "sanctification" means to be set apart from the world for God. If you want to be used by God, you cannot flirt with the world. If you want God to be able to minister through you, then you cannot afford to "fool around" with the world or "take it easy" like the world does. You cannot afford this, in spite of what others may do.

We do not separate ourselves from this world because God does not want us to have any fun. We separate ourselves from this world because we want to be used by the Holy Spirit. We are so concentrated on what God wants us to do, that we do not have time to defile our minds with worldly, ungodly films and videos.

We do not relax in the flesh or go on a backsliding vacation. God is our source in everything and the best relaxation we can find is to devote ourselves to Him and to enjoy basking in His presence.

And he will turn many of the children of Israel to the Lord their God. He will also go before Him in the spirit and power of Elijah, 'to turn the hearts of the fathers to the children,' and the disobedient to the wisdom of the just, to **make ready a people prepared for the Lord** (Luke 1:16-17).

The strength of the prophet's ministry lies in his ability to break through to the point that even the unrepentant, those who do not hear and will not listen, have their consciences pricked so that they suddenly respond. There is a time when people who otherwise refuse to hear, truly begin to listen. However, this will not happen if we run out into the street shouting "Sanas just had an earthquake and now the whole world is coming to an end." The world merely laughs and ridicules such antics.

On the other hand, there is an anointing which penetrates people's hearts so that, although they may be disobedient, they are seized by it and compelled to say, "What must we do?" This will not happen by scolding them, or behaving in a fleshly, hard and arrogant manner toward them. It will happen when you speak under a prophetic anointing that stings their consciences.

This is exactly what occurred under the ministry of John the Baptist. People's lives were changed and they turned out in full force from Jerusalem and the region around the Jordan to be baptized by him. What had been said of John prophetically—that he would turn *the disobedient to the wisdom of the just, to make ready a people prepared for the Lord—had been fulfilled.*

John preached repentance: "Repent," he declared, "for the kingdom of heaven is at hand!" (Matt 3:2).

But when he saw many of the Pharisees and Sadducees coming to his baptism, he said to them, "Brood of vipers! Who has warned you to flee from the wrath to come?...And even now the axe is laid to the root of the trees. Therefore every tree which does not bear good fruit is cut down and thrown into the fire" (Matt 3:7,10).

A prophet always preaches against sin. Just as the evangelist is passionate about salvation, signs and wonders, so the prophet has an all-consuming passion for purity, more so than any other ministry office. The evangelist is especially concerned with signs and wonders. He thinks about them and lives in them. He rejoices when he sees people's backs straightened, new eyes created and sicknesses disappear. This is his life. In the same way, the prophet is consumed with purity.

It is distressing to see a pastor compromise, but because he has such a heart for people, he is tempted to turn a blind eye to their sin. It is just as distressing for the evangelist to compromise. In order to win or reach more people, the evangelist may avoid preaching certain truths. This is his area of weakness. The teacher also has the chance to compromise, but it is worst of all, when the prophet compromises.

It is a very serious thing before God when a prophet, who is called to preach against sin, lives in sin personally or sees the sin of others, without doing anything about it. It has serious consequences for all of us, but especially for the one who has this unique calling and anointing on his life.

For if God did not spare the natural branches, he may not spare you either. Therefore consider the goodness and severity of God: on those who fell, severity; but toward you, goodness. Otherwise you also will be cut off (Rom 11:21-22).

Mercy and Judgment

Some prophets do not want to be associated with judgment. "I am not a prophet of doom," they say. "I am a prophet of grace." Yet, this is not a true statement. God is both a God of mercy and of judgment. He is loving, holy, righteous and almighty. He encompasses all these attributes. He is good to those who humble themselves and stern with those who refuse to submit.

John the Baptist called the Pharisees a brood of vipers! (Matt 3:7). He knew that they and the Sadducees refused to submit themselves to God because they were proud and stiff-necked. However, he spoke differently to the people themselves. To those who humbled themselves and asked, "What should we do?" he replied, "Repent and be baptized."

In other words, the prophetic anointing is kind, loving, merciful and full of grace toward those who desire to follow Jesus wholeheartedly. But to those who are stiff-necked and hard-hearted and do not want to follow Jesus, it is like a hammer and a sword, displaying the severity of God. The wrath and judgment of God are a result of His nature.

If someone with the calling of a prophet prophesies only prosperity, success and happiness, although these things can be prophesied in the Holy Spirit, there is a possibility that he has compromised.

We are living at the end of one age and we will soon see the beginning of another. Even the devil is prophesying about this, actually calling it the New Age. Those within the New Age Movement claim that preparations need to be made for the new age which is soon to come. Then, a world leader will arise who will appear good and kind, and everyone will listen to him. This leader will create peace here on earth.

These people are openly talking about the Antichrist, throughout the world today. They even occasionally go so far as to call him the devil, and sometimes even Lucifer. They explain that the new age is coming but that there are those who oppose it, describing these people as old-fashioned and awkward, standing in the way of change. They are referring to the "fundamentalists"— Christians who stubbornly cling to the Bible as God's infallible Word.

An ungodly government, may pay attention to these "New Age prophets of peace and prosperity," who have found an easy entrance into the business world by offering courses and other activities; but the Church will continue to preach the Word of God.

Even if 450 "prophets of Baal" prophesy prosperity and success, reassuring us that all the answers will be found when we "discover ourselves" and our "inner light" and "inner strength," we will continue to prophesy truth and declare what God says.

And God never says that man intrinsically, has the Godhead within him or that he himself is a god.

God says that without Him, man is a sinner on the road to destruction, but that there is forgiveness for his sins through the blood of Jesus. By receiving Jesus as his Lord and Savior, a man can be saved and become a child of God. Every man and woman can be born again by faith in what Jesus has accomplished on the cross, by confessing Jesus as Lord and receiving Him into their hearts. They then become a new creation in Christ Jesus and the Holy Spirit comes to dwell within them.

Without Jesus, man is lost. But through Him and His reconciliatory work on Calvary, man can be saved by grace—not by his own good deeds—when he freely accepts and receives by faith what Jesus has done for him on the cross.

In the days to come it will be increasingly important for us to hold fast to the fundamentals of the Gospel, no matter how old-fashioned it may sound to New Age ears. Only Jesus saves. Only the Gospel is the power of God.

9

The Foundation, the Way and the Goal

The ministry of the prophet is a *foundational ministry*. He is most involved in building churches, partly to prepare the Bride for the Bridegroom and partly to minister guidance, instruction, exhortation, judgment and revelation to the church.

Leading and guidance means that the prophet has the ability to see and convey direction to individuals and churches, and even to the entire Body of Christ. He knows what the next step is and how to prepare for it. This is the prophet's unique calling and anointing and we must listen to what he says—especially since it can put an entire church on the proper course. In the midst of confusion, the voice of God is heard and direction is given to the church.

The prophet may bring instruction in an unusual and different way than the teacher. His instruction comes through prophetic preaching and teaching. Perhaps like no other, the prophet is able to exhort, correct, challenge, encourage and provoke. He also has an ability in God to deliver warnings and judgments. He is able to discern a spiritual climate and convey God's viewpoint on an issue.

Jesus was very powerful in this ministry. What looked good to others, He could call *whitewashed tombs which indeed appear beautiful outwardly, but inside are full of dead men's bones and all uncleanness* (Matt 23:27).

The prophet operates in revelation, both present and future, both personal and general.

The prophetic anointing says, "I see it, I see it!" as God tells the prophet, "This is where we are going." This vision of the overall objective then colors his entire being. People need to know where they are going, but the prophet does not stop there, he also tells them how to get there.

The Goal—And the Way to Get There

The Lord may tell a church that one day they will have 10,000 members. "Hallelujah," says the visionary, "that's great, let's all go home and have a cup of coffee!" Anyone, can have a big vision. You do not need to be a prophet for that.

In the same way, anyone can rejoice about having a giant church, but what happens when all hell breaks loose and half of the members leave the church and the devil says, "Just look at things now. Perhaps the Lord does not keep His promises. It might take Him a little while to come through!"

In the last days, scoffers will come and say, *Where is the promise of His coming? For since the fathers fell asleep, all things continue as they were from the beginning of creation* (2 Pet 3:3-4).

The same scoffers were there to mock Noah after he had prophesied about the coming flood. Noah was saying, "It's going to rain and there will be a great flood."

But the people merely asked, "What is rain?" They had never even heard of rain before. "So you're building an ark on the land, up in the mountains. Wouldn't it be better to build it next to a lake?" they asked.

"No," said Noah, "there is a flood coming and it's coming soon. When I have finished building I will get inside the ark and you are all going to drown."

No one believed Noah. The people just laughed at him. They pulled his beard and kicked at the ark—until the day the water finally came. Suddenly, their laughter turned to terror. The mockery, the joking, the arrogance, the worldliness and the backsliding were drowned and everything grew strangely quiet. The promise of God was fulfilled. Everyone could have built their own little ark, but no one built, except the one who had received the word from God.

God also spoke to Moses and said, "Go and deliver my people! The children of Israel are to leave Egypt and you, Moses, are their deliverer! You are the one who will lead the people out." Moses was overjoyed, but Pharaoh was not, and Moses met with fierce resistance.

Many people receive a mighty revelation and have powerful prophecies spoken over them, but eventually, they become miserable and wish that they had never received a prophecy in the first place. They fail to see that a prophecy is a vision of what is to come and it must be accompanied by revelation on how to get there. If people refuse to take the path specified by the Holy Spirit—if they refuse to clear up and clean out their lives and make changes in accordance with His directives—they will never see what He has spoken come to pass.

Hold Fast to the Word!

People often fail to realize that the thrill over the fact that God has spoken to them gradually disappears, and the feeling of being someone important fades. Then the devil, who has also heard the word, tries everything within his power to snatch it away from you. Things may get difficult and troublesome. If this makes you upset and angry, or if you sit at home whining and complaining and feeling sorry for yourself, then you are just a spiritual baby.

We have all been like this at some point, but we are all growing in God. We must come to the place where we stop being frustrated, self-centered and complaining to God all the time, and instead start believing the prophecies we have heard and adjust our lives accordingly. When we take the prophetic word seriously, begin to act on it and obey the instructions we receive, we will reach our goal. *Believe His prophets, and you shall prosper* (2 Chron 20:20).

"Pharaoh" may rise up against you and say, "I'm never going to let you go. You will never make it into your ministry." Have you ever heard that before? However, if God has called you to something you can reply, "I'm not just waiting to be what God has called me to be; in God I already am! By faith I have already received it!"

The prophetic word is just as real before it becomes manifest, as it will be when it does manifest in the future. If God has said something, it will be so. You need to take seriously the word you have received, begin to confess it and use the sword of the Spirit against Satan in order to chase him away from your path. You will soon discover that believing in the prophetic message will cause you to prosper.

Everything will happen just as God has said, but do not be foolish enough to believe that it will happen overnight. Many have stumbled over the prophetic message by wrongly expecting it to be fulfilled immediately. Either that, or they had decided how and through whom it would come to pass, which is clearly wrong.

There was nothing wrong with what God said. If you hold fast to it, it will eventually be fulfilled.

10

The Prophet Activates Gifts and Ministries

The prophet activates ministries and gifts. He has the *ability to see God's gifts and callings over people's lives,* although he does not see these things over everyone's life. Therefore, it is best not to approach a prophet and ask him to tell you what your ministry is and what he sees over you. It is not necessary to run after prophets in an effort to find out everything; doing so is unsound and immature.

Instead, you should simply do what you are called to do and God will confirm your calling, through prophetic ministries. They will see the calling on your life and the gifts within you that you yourself may not even have discovered. They are there, slumbering in your spirit, and the prophetic word takes hold of them, brings them to the surface, and activates them!

Both the apostle and the prophet possess this special ability. In fact, when you examine the apostle and the prophet in the New Testament, you will notice that they traveled together in groups, in apostolic teams.

In the Old Testament, there were disciples who followed the prophets, as well as schools for prophets. However, I believe that the place for the training of prophets in the New Testament is the church. Here, the people can learn to flow in the Holy Spirit and hear from God. Even the prophet needs to stay in contact with the local church.

Expect Words from Heaven

The prophet's task is to train and encourage. He has the ability to see your gift, bring it forth, and in the spirit, train you and send you out into service for God.

On several occasions, prophetic messages have completely revolutionalized my life and have shown me the right direction. They have come directly from God just at a time in my life when a critical decision had to be made.

At every critical or significant point in your life, you should expect the Lord to speak to you prophetically. However, you need not pray to receive a prophecy for every little day-to-day decision. We are not spiritists. The gifts we are talking about operate precisely in the spirit, but are not to be confused with occultism.

Neither do we need to act as they did in the Old Covenant, running to the prophet, the king or the priest at every available opportunity. Unlike most people in the Old Testament, you have the Spirit of God and you are able to hear from heaven personally. However, the prophet is a part of the New Covenant, and there is nothing wrong with asking for his counsel. But it is wrong if you become dependent on consulting him before you can do anything.

CHARACTERISTICS
OF THE PROPHET

11

The Prophet—God's X-ray Vision

Now when He was in Jerusalem at the Passover, during the feast, many believed in His name when they saw the signs which He did. But Jesus did not commit Himself to them, because He knew all men, and had no need that anyone should testify of man, for He knew what was in man (John 2:23-25).

The prophet has *the ability to know the intents and purposes of men's hearts* more than anyone else. This is why a prophet can be somewhat intimidating. There is something about the prophet which evokes respect from people and can make them feel slightly nervous; some folks may even keep themselves at a distance. Prophets can give the impression that they see right through you, and this can produce feelings of insecurity about what they might discover.

However, a prophet sees nothing unless God reveals it to him. And God does not reveal everything about everyone all the time. The prophet cannot see everything, besides, he would never be able to bear it if he did. He would probably become like Elijah, sitting under the juniper tree saying, "I want to go home to heaven. They are backslidden, everyone of them."

The prophetic anointing leads people to repent quickly. It turns the hearts of the fathers to the children and the hearts of the children to their fathers. It evokes an awesome respect in some people, and a hatred and contempt in others. When the prophet speaks, it is so clearly on behalf of the Lord that everything becomes either black or white. People are given a choice between either heaven or hell. Rebellion rises up in those who refuse to choose, while those who are humble and who submit to God, are set free.

See the Motives

He who hates, disguises it with his lips, and lays up deceit within himself; when he speaks kindly, do not believe him, for there are seven abominations in his heart; though his hatred is covered by deceit, his wickedness will be revealed before the assembly (Prov 26:24-26).

Hatred, deceit, guile, falsehood and wickedness can be concealed in the church and in people's lives, until, that is, they are revealed. The prophetic ministry operates powerfully in this kind of revelation. No one is able to see into the hearts of people like the prophet.

Peter operated in a powerful prophetic anointing when he exposed the deceit of Ananias and Sapphira (see Acts 5:1-11). Most pastors would have been thrilled with the couple and the evangelist would have been happy to receive their financial support—but not the apostle or the prophet.

Peter was an apostle in the office of a prophet. He was used prophetically to usher in the New Covenant. He received a revelation telling him to kill and eat, and he later understood that it was not necessary to become a Jew in order to be a Christian. He was used as a forerunner of the New Covenant.

Later, as pastor of the church, he received a prophetic anointing and the gift of discerning of spirits. He saw the deceit in Ananias and Sapphira, recognizing that the candy-coated exterior was hiding the fact that Satan had filled their hearts.

If a church wants to grow strong, the believers must live in the light rather than merely pretending and in reality, living as hypocrites. The prophetic word must have room to flow, even in exposing hidden wickedness, guile, slander, rebellion and criticism.

The prophet must be able to reveal the contents of those people's hearts who have determined to turn from following the truth, and are hindering and ruining life for others. These people may claim that all is well, but a simple application of the Word shows that this is far from the case.

This is why the office of the prophet is feared by many and even hated by some. However, if the prophet is permitted to operate as he should, the result will be blessing. He clears out, cleans up, puts in order and points the way like no other ministry gift can.

Repent therefore and be converted, that your sins may be blotted out, so that times of refreshing may come from the presence of the Lord, and that He may send Jesus Christ, who was preached to you before, whom heaven must receive until the times of restoration of all things, which God has spoken by the mouth of all His holy prophets since the world began (Acts 3:19-21).

God spoke to His prophets and revealed His plan; that Jesus Christ would come to the earth and later return again. Times of refreshing would come upon those who believed in Him until the restoration of all things.

Watchmen on the Walls

Wherever there is a powerful, growing church, God will send people to it who need to be built up and made strong. For this reason, if you are not a part of a local church, you should join one.

But just as God leads people to join a local church, so the devil would also like certain people to join. He would very much like to get the people who serve his purposes to join the church, to disrupt and tear down all that God is working to build up.

When the pastor receives people into the church, he has a generous attitude and says, "Of course brother so-and-so can join the church. He'll get that thing sorted out and everything will be just fine." He opens his heart to welcome him in.

The prophet's heart is not always so welcoming, although the heart of God is there. The prophet looks at motives. He sees why people come to the church, why they want to help, and so on. This is incredibly important for the churches of the coming decade, because many will come, all with different motives and different reasons.

People will come who simply love Jesus and desire to have the nurturing and protection provided by the local church. There will be people who come in straight out of the world with lives full of worldliness, problems and misery, who are merely looking for help. Jesus loves them and desires to cleanse, deliver and help them in every way.

However, in addition to these people, there will also be those with impure motives. They may not be as serious as Ananias and Sapphira, but they exemplify this kind of person well. They always want to be the center of attention, surrounded by followers. They want to sit right at the front of the church rather than at the back. If they really had their way, they would get up on the stage and take over the whole meeting.

In active churches, which will invariably meet with this type of problem, the prophet is needed to act as a watchman who stands on the walls and keeps a careful lookout. A watchman is extremely important in the local church. It might be an intercessor with a prophetic anointing, a prophetic spirit resting on an ordinary believer, or prophets in the church who are posted on the wall. Any one of these may keep guard on the wall, watching and spying.

There were watchmen posted on the walls in the Old Testament. When they saw the enemy approaching they sent a messenger to the king. The same is true for the local church; the one who watches must also *communicate* what he sees and hears in the spirit. This is something often neglected by the prophet. At times he is so caught up with his own thoughts and experiences, that he completely forgets the true purpose of what God has told him to do.

God Always Has a Way Out

If we begin to compromise and let various types of sin into our churches, our strength will leave and our anointing will depart. But if we then repent and cry out to God, He is there with His power to help us. The story of Israel in the Old Testament is one long account of how they fell into sin, were restored and then fell once more. Time and time again, God sent His servants the prophets to talk sense into His people.

In Judges 6 we find them facing one of their defeats, the enemy having got the better of them.

So Israel was greatly impoverished because of the Midianites, and the children of Israel cried out to the Lord.

And it came to pass, when the children of Israel cried out to the Lord because of the Midianites, that the Lord sent a prophet to the children of Israel, who said to them, "Thus says the Lord God of Israel: 'I brought you up from Egypt and brought you out of the house of bondage; and I delivered you out of the hand of the Egyptians and out of the hand of all who oppressed you, and drove them out before you and gave you their land. Also I said to you, I am the Lord your God; do not fear the gods of the Amorites, in whose land you dwell. But you have not obeyed My voice'" (Judg 6:6-10).

Israel ended up in a state of misery and then cried out to God. When they did, He sent them a prophet whose task was to analyze the situation, look at the x-ray plates and

103

say, "It's cancer!" The prophet can be likened to God's x-ray vision. He diagnoses the problem and identifies the solution.

After the prophet had delivered God's solution to the problem and His divine direction for the future, God sent an angel to another man, Gideon. He was a warrior of the Lord and the man whom God chose to carry out the plan that had already been prepared by the prophetic word of the prophet.

This illustrates how the apostle and the prophet work in conjunction with one another. The prophet has a unique ministry that sees things in the spirit more precisely than any other. But the apostle possesses a greater authority and impact when it comes to executing God's plans. The prophet does not necessarily have to carry out all that he has prophesied.

The apostle has an unequaled ability, not only in prophesying the counsels of God, but in taking hold of those counsels, of that revelation, and using them as a sledgehammer to bring lasting change. This is the primary difference between the functions of the apostle and the prophet, and in this way they complement and cooperate with one another.

Every prophetic message, *always points to a way out,* even if it brings heavy judgment. There is always a way out when God speaks. No matter how many sins may have been committed, a way of escape is always presented.

However, the devil *never* offers a way out when he speaks. He offers only hopelessness, meaninglessness and misery. There is a feeling of general powerlessness, and it is difficult to really identify what is wrong; you just have a feeling that there is something wrong. "There must be something wrong with me," we think.

This is the way our enemy talks to us. He brings condemnation, he is unspecific and he engulfs people in a cloud of hopelessness, confusion, desperation and self-contempt. You should never listen to this.

Concrete Reasons for Defeat

If you love Jesus, your starting point is one of victory. If you desire to follow Him on His terms, then you are in a winning position. Victory is normal.

Victory was commonplace for Joshua. When he marched against Ai and the children of Israel were defeated, he was perplexed and dismayed. He was used to winning. He was accustomed to having God with them. But this time, God said to Joshua:

Get up! Why do you lie thus on your face? Israel has sinned, and they have also transgressed My covenant which I commanded them. For they have even taken some of the accursed things, and have both stolen and deceived; and they have also put it among their own stuff. **Therefore** the children of Israel could not stand before their enemies, but turned their backs before their enemies, because they have become doomed to destruction. Neither will I be with you anymore, unless you destroy the accursed from among you. Get up, sanctify the people, and say, "Sanctify yourselves for tomorrow, because thus says the Lord God of Israel: 'There is an accursed thing in your midst, O Israel; you cannot stand before your enemies until you take away the accursed thing **from among you**'" (Josh 7:10-13).

The Holy Spirit had spoken and shown Joshua what was wrong and had also given him the answer to their difficulties. The Spirit of God always gives us a solution— if we want it, that is.

Even when His messages are serious, God does not intend to oppress people. He never comes to condemn. He may come in power and say, "Sin is in the camp!" Then you know the truth; you feel convicted and stung as God tells you, "Get rid of that!" If you receive this correction you will be relieved.

105

God is specific and He is always full of encouragement. Even if it comes in the form of a warning or judgment, it always results in restoration, greater purity, greater freedom, more strength, more joy and more power.

12

Opposition to the Prophetic Office

One of the first things we notice about the prophetic ministry, which is perhaps alarming, is the unequaled opposition shown toward this ministry. The prophet, and even the apostle, meet with greater resistance than any of the other ministry gifts.

When this opposition is viewed on the surface, it is important to interpret it correctly rather than letting the flesh interpret its meaning. Some tend to think that if a great deal of controversy surrounds something, then it must be wrong. But this is not necessarily the case. Perhaps there is so much controversy because it is right. You must dare to think a little differently.

This does not imply that it you hear negative comments about something, then there is automatically something right about it. However, if you take, for example, the apostle Paul and the prophet and teacher Silas, you will notice that commotion followed them wherever they went. It was said of them: *These who have turned the world upside down have come here too* (Acts 17:6).

The spirit world shook when they came because their function was to establish. In the church today, the apostle and prophet also have an *establishing* function, as well as a *reformative* one. The enemy does not take kindly to this, and consequently, he is out to attack these ministries. As a result, God has given the apostle and the prophet a unique ability to break through in the spirit realm.

Not every prophet is like Jeremiah. Neither are they all like John the Baptist. It is not necessary to dress in camel's hair or eat grasshoppers in order to be a prophet!

There is a wide variation within the prophetic office. Samuel was the first prophet after Moses and for this reason, reference is often made in the New Testament to "Samuel and the prophets." Samuel always spoke to the people of Israel, and was their leader. He experienced little persecution in the sense that we have just mentioned.

Of course, Saul was against him, so he did meet with resistance, but overall, he had a different function from that of the other prophets. He instructed the people; visiting the various towns of Israel, judging, administering justice and speaking the word of the Lord to them.

As we consider the prophetic ministry, we must avoid creating a stereotype image of what a prophet should be. A prophet needs freedom to become the person God has called him to be. He needs freedom to minister as God instructs him, so that all that God desires to accomplish can be fulfilled.

Count on Opposition

Every prophet, and every individual who wishes to serve God, will meet with opposition. Mark 4 clearly tells us that persecution comes for the sake of the Word. This kind of pressure will come against every believer and so, we need to learn how to deal with it.

The prophet will experience this opposition. People may not always immediately receive or understand his message, although eventually they will. However, in some cases this can take a long time. People may even fail to comprehend his message while he is still alive. We can see a recurrent pattern throughout history—as soon as prophets die they are called saints. The very people who stoned them use those same stones to build a monument to them when they are gone.

Jesus stood in each of the five ministry offices. He was an apostle, prophet, evangelist, pastor and teacher. In Luke 4 the Bible gives us an account of what happened one day when the Spirit of the Lord had come on Him and He stood in the synagogue, reading from the Word of God and prophesying.

And He began to say to them, "Today this scripture is fulfilled in your hearing."

So all bore witness to Him, and marveled at the gracious words which proceeded out of His mouth. And they said, "Is this not Joseph's son?" And He said to them, "You will surely say this proverb to Me, 'Physician, heal yourself! Whatever we have heard done in Capernaum, do also here in Your country.' " Then He said, "Assuredly, I say to you, no prophet is accepted in his own country. "But I tell you truly, many widows were in Israel in the days of Elijah, when the heaven was shut up three years and six months, and there was a great famine throughout all the land; but to none of them was Elijah sent except to Zarephath, in the region of Sidon, to a woman who was a widow. And many lepers were in Israel in the time of Elijah the prophet, and none of them was cleansed except Naaman the Syrian." Then all those in the synagogue, when they heard these things, were filled with wrath, and rose up and thrust Him out of the city; and they led Him to the brow of the hill on which their city was built, that they might throw Him down over the cliff (Luke 4:21-29).

The prophetic word was immediately confirmed. It took no more than five seconds for them to do exactly what Jesus had said. What had Jesus said? That a prophet is without honor in his own country.

So they were offended at Him. But Jesus said to them, "A prophet is not without honor except in his own country and in his own house." And He did not do many mighty works there because of their unbelief (Matt 13:57-58).

There are three areas mentioned here in which a prophet can expect opposition. The first is his own country, the second is his home town and the third is his own household, or his family. In other words, Jesus is saying: You can count on resistance everywhere!

Remember that Jesus even turned to one of His disciples and said, *Get behind Me, Satan! You are an offence to Me, for you are not mindful of the things of God, but the things of men* (Matt 16:23). Even in Jesus' immediate surroundings there was sudden opposition toward the prophetic anointing and revelation that He had.

He came to His own, and His own did not receive Him. But as many as received Him, to them He gave the right to become children of God (John 1:11-12). There is often a contempt for revelation, the prophetic word, simplicity, sincerity, innocence and purity.

Pure and Simple

The prophet is consumed with purity. However, it is impossible to be pure without simplicity. The prophets were able to accomplish all that they did because they were simple and they were sincere. Their simplicity meant that they were wholehearted. They were not divided or double-minded having one attitude in public and another in private. Simplicity is being straightforward, open and genuine.

When you are simple and open and concentrate on loving Jesus, it will attract people who are seeking God, while simultaneously producing contempt in those who have no desire to approach Him. When the Word of God goes forth in purity, it divides between soul and spirit and is a judge of the thoughts and intents of the heart (Heb 4:12).

Therefore, Jesus was made a sign that some might believe on Him (see Luke 2:34). Those who do, will never be put to shame (1 Pet 2:6). However, to those who refused to believe in Him, Jesus became a stumbling block that confounded them (Matt 13:57-58).

Pride stumbles on the prophetic word, and when it does, it also begins to belittle prophecy. Jesus says that if you enter a prophetic ministry, you must be prepared to meet contempt, opposition and misunderstanding. This is true even for the members of your own household, or for those close to you in your hometown or country. If you are prepared for this, you will be able to handle opposition and persecution successfully when it comes.

Be free from every form of persecution complex. Train yourself to have a spirit of excellence. You should be like Daniel, who was a prophet and a statesman. He was second in charge to the Babylonian king and was surrounded by a large number of astrologers, strange soothsayers, magicians and all kinds of occult phenomena.

Daniel was surrounded by many people who plotted against him, spoke out curses and tried to remove him from office. Difficulties and attacks were a common occurrence, but he just continued to see visions and receive revelations. No one was able to touch him.

They passed a law making it illegal to pray, but Daniel prayed anyway. They threw him into the lion's den and the gift of faith came into immediate operation in his life. He told the lions to be quiet and then lay down to sleep and woke up the next morning.

No trace of self-pity or persecution complex was found in Daniel. He walked with God.

In Matthew 23, Jesus pronounces seven woes over the Pharisees. He calls them blind guides, fools, blind Pharisees, whitewashed tombs, snakes and a brood of vipers. I have never heard a preacher get all these things into one sermon. However, Jesus did.

There are those who say, "Some preachers are so hard." But if you read about Jesus, you will soon discover that He was much harder. How could He be so categorical? How could He possibly say such things? Because He was pure and free; He was without selfish motives.

John 5:30 says that Jesus does not make His own judgments: *As I hear, I judge; and My judgment is righteous, because I do not seek My own will but the will of the Father who sent Me.* Jesus has no underlying motives in what He says.

The Hatred of Phariseeism

A prophet must not give in to the temptation to prophesy things that he would simply like to take the opportunity to say. There are countless examples, in churches and in other contexts, of people who have simply controlled others through "prophecies." This kind of practice is extremely dangerous and violates the will of God. You need to be able to discern between true prophecy and what is just general chatter.

If a person has been entrusted with the Word of the Lord, he cannot merely prophesy based on personal preference and opinion. If you begin to prophesy your personal opinions over people's lives, you will cause chaos and be partly responsible for their failures. You need to make sure that you are free from disappointment, persecution complexes, soulish ambitions and all that has to do with self, so that you are surrendered to Jesus and do only what He tells you to do.

Jesus was pure and free in relation to Himself. This made it possible for God to give Him the necessary authority and strength to tell the Pharisees seven times what they had in their hearts. When He said these things, it was done in a spirit of revelation, purity, truth and love and without the involvement of fleshly reactions.

Therefore, indeed, I send you prophets, wise men,
some of them you will kill and crucify, and some of
scourge in your synagogues and persecute from c..,
on you may come all the righteous blood shed on the earth, ...
the blood of righteous Abel to the blood of Zechariah, son of
Berechiah, whom you murdered between the temple and the
altar. Assuredly, I say to you, all these things will come upon this
generation. O Jerusalem, Jerusalem, the one who kills the
prophets and stones those who are sent to her! How often I
wanted to gather your children together, as a hen gathers her
chicks under her wings, but you were not willing! See! Your
house is left to you desolate (Matt 23:34-38).

What is Jerusalem? It is a religious headquarters. Where
people are no longer in the spirit, where there has been
spiritual decay and religious politics have prevailed; then
what used to be a center for the Gospel becomes a
stronghold of religiosity. The next thing that happens in
this situation is that the prophets are killed.

In the eyes of God, the opposition created by the enemy
through backslidden religiosity, is by far the worst. Here,
the enemy has succeeded in infiltrating Christians with
something that prevents them from finding truth and
freedom. This same spirit was over Jezebel, who killed the
prophets wherever she happened to find them. This spirit
holds people in religious bondage, far away from truth,
reality and freedom.

The greatest resistance to the Gospel is to be found in
religious circles rather than in the world. Unsaved people
are often either apathetic or questioning and curious
toward the Gospel. Usually the greatest opposition, the
most slander and the strongest rebellion come from the
religious sector.

In one of his books, C.S. Lewis says that nothing is quite
as dangerous as a Pharisee and that no hatred is as fierce as
theological hatred from those who have lost the life of God,

departed from fellowship with Him and are left only with empty doctrines.

The same is true of those who have compromised with doctrine and departed from the Word of God, who then meet someone who still displays God's life and walks in obedience. Their hearts are often ignited with hatred—if they refuse to receive the truth, that is—and they operate in the spirit of Cain.

What did Cain do? He was so enraged by the fact that God accepted Abel and his offering that he killed Abel. This is the same spirit that Jesus talks about in Matthew 23. It began to operate in Cain and continued right up to those who killed Zechariah, the son of Berechiah. That same spirit was in the world when Jesus came. John says that He came to His own but that His own did not receive Him (John 1:11).

Because of this same spirit, Jesus pronounces the woes over the Pharisees and speaks to Jerusalem saying, *O Jerusalem, Jerusalem, the one who kills the prophets....*

13

Special Relationship— Special Protection

"For behold, I have made you this day A fortified city and an iron pillar, And bronze walls against the whole land—Against the kings of Judah, Against its princes, Against its priests, And against the people of the land. They will fight against you, But they shall not prevail against you, For I am with you," says the Lord, "to deliver you" (Jer 1:18-19).

No other ministry is as dependent on an intimate relationship with God as the prophetic ministry. The prophet is in desperate need of God's protection and help. This is because he occasionally brings revelations and truth which, are slightly uncomfortable. There may be times when he wishes he had been an evangelist or a teacher instead, but this is not for him to decide. God said to Jeremiah: *Before you were born I sanctified you; I ordained you a prophet to the nations* (Jer 1:5).

At the same time that God called Jeremiah, He also gave him a special word, one that applies to all prophets. "I myself will help you," God told him. "Even if the whole country, the whole kingdom and all those who surround you are against you, I will be with you."

This is not the general principle that Jesus gave us when He promised to be with us always, even to the end of the age. It is an intimate relationship experienced by the prophet between himself and God. Of course, there is a

115

danger that this kind of relationship can go to the prophet's head so that he begins to feel exclusive and elite.

On the other hand, however, when it is functioning properly it is a special relationship that offers special protection. God Himself watches over and protects His prophet so that he does not need to run home and compromise, but is prepared to take the consequences of the message he delivers.

Supernatural Protection

When they were few in number, Indeed very few, and strangers in it. When they went from one nation to another, from one kingdom to another people, He permitted no one to do them wrong; Yes, He rebuked kings for their sakes, saying, "Do not touch My anointed ones, And do My prophets no harm" (Ps 105:12-15).

At times people have misapplied this scripture. The fact that you are in leadership in a church does not automatically make you infallible. It does not mean that people are not allowed to question or examine anything you say. You should not try to hide behind the scripture that says, "Touch not the Lord's anointed."

Every minister makes mistakes. There are always things that need to be discussed and clarified. The question is simply in which spirit this is done. A worldly person cannot understand this. Every church must allow room for various stages and levels of faith.

It is normal to wonder about things, and people can and are allowed, to make mistakes. There must be room for this in every church. At the same time, there must be a respect for the fact that God actually speaks through His servants to the church and that His Word must be obeyed if the church is to be blessed.

When God uses His prophets, His servants and His people, He very clearly says, "Do not touch them, they are my mouthpieces. I use them and if you touch them, I will touch you." His servants are so closely identified with the message of God that it is not just they who are doing the talking; it is God Himself speaking through them. So by attacking them, one is really attacking God.

This is something that we sometimes find difficult to accept, because of our humanistic, worldly way of thinking. Due to our rebellious nature, we have difficulty accepting the fact that men and women, anointed by the Holy Spirit, can actually speak on God's behalf.

Supernatural protection is provided for those who do speak on the Lord's behalf. The words they speak are not open to discussion, argument or assessment. We can test it and see whether or not it is a prophetic word, but the moment we know in our hearts that it is from God, we can no longer resist it. We must then receive it as something from heaven.

The Safest Place

And when he was in the Gate of Benjamin, a captain of the guard was there whose name was Irijah the son of Shelemiah, the son of Hananiah; and he seized Jeremiah the prophet, saying, "You are defecting to the Chaldeans!" Then Jeremiah said, "False! I am not defecting to the Chaldeans." But he did not listen to him. So Irijah seized Jeremiah and brought him to the princes. Therefore the princes were angry with Jeremiah, and they struck him and put him in prison in the house of Jonathan the scribe. For they had made that the prison (Jer 37:13-15).

This false accusation against Jeremiah came because he was being courageous enough to say what God said, even when everyone else was saying the opposite. After being thrown into prison, we might have expected him to soften up a little, change his mind and begin to compromise; but not Jeremiah.

When Jeremiah entered the dungeon, and the cells, and Jeremiah had remained there many days, then Zedekiah the king sent and took him out. The king asked him secretly in his house, and said, "Is there any word from the Lord?" And Jeremiah said, "There is." Then he said, "You shall be delivered into the hand of the king of Babylon!" (Jer 37:16-17)

The strange thing is that after publicly defaming Jeremiah and having thrown him into prison, they secretly came to him and asked, "Have you heard anything from the Lord, by any chance?"

Jeremiah is an excellent example of a true prophet of doom. He stood alone against the entire nation. Although he sat in a dungeon he became even stronger. He was not tempted by the opportunity to flatter the king when he was brought before him again. Jeremiah could easily have adjusted his previous message; just corrected it slightly and got himself out of prison. Instead, when the king asked for a word, he was even bolder.

Moreover Jeremiah said to King Zedekiah, "What offence have I committed against you, against your servants, or against this people, that you have put me in prison? Where now are your prophets who prophesied to you, saying, 'The king of Babylon will not come against you or against this land?' " (Jer 37:18-19)

Jeremiah's words came to pass exactly. However, he remained in prison and, strangely enough, this very dungeon served to protect him when Jerusalem was captured. When the battle was over, Jeremiah was a free man. God preserved him in a remarkable way because he had refused to compromise. He was prepared to take the consequences of the message God had given him. Therefore God provided him with special protection.

Although Jerusalem was destroyed and in chaos, Jeremiah survived unharmed, and he remained free. Then, as a free man, he was able to sit on the ruins of Jerusalem and write the book of Lamentations. He looked out over the desolate, ruined city and prophesied over it.

As a servant of the Lord, you will receive the most effective protection by being closest to the front line. Of course, you will also find the greatest opposition here. Many people consider such resistance too difficult, but just remember David. Things went well for him as long as he led his armies into battle. But the day he gave this responsibility to others, left the front line and stayed at home in his royal palace was the day he noticed Bathsheba and subsequently fell into sin.

Your best protection is always to be on the front line and at the forefront of what God is doing. If God gives you a powerful message, He will also provide you with powerful protection. Always remember that. God does not want things to go wrong for you; His desire is that everything goes well in your life. You do not need to change His message. Just say what He wants you to say and let God take the consequences—and He will.

14

A Long-Term Strategist

The office of the prophet *works with a long-range perspective.* He speaks out things that only a few people really understand. Much of what he says seems odd and unusual, and some of it may not be fulfilled until after his death. Perhaps more than the other ministry gifts, his ministry works on a long-term time scale.

We all know how it can be with us human beings—especially with those of us who claim to walk in faith. We are, paradoxically enough, terribly dependent on what we see! The point of faith teaching is to tell us not to be so dependent on what we see, hear and feel, but in spite of this, it is easy to become dependent on our senses. We have a constant desire to see and feel something.

However, the prophet, works with a wide perspective. It may seem as though nothing happens or takes place that is of any significance. When he prophesies something, the opposite almost seems to occur, and he is left standing there feeling embarrassed.

However, if the whole time perspective is taken into consideration, it is plain to see that things have turned out precisely as God had said they would, through His servants, the prophets.

That is why it says in the New Testament: *God, who at various times and in various ways spoke in time past to the fathers by the prophets* (Heb 1:1), and, *As He spoke by the*

121

mouth of His holy prophets (Luke 1:70). Here, God rightly emphasizes the fact that what He had spoken through the prophets hundreds, almost thousands of years ago, has actually come to pass.

The prophet must struggle *with this aspect of time* and the fact that his words not offer immediate dividends. Certain ministries see immediate results while others have to wait a little longer. At this point, *patience* is needed in order not to give up, back down or become depressed.

Bronze Walls and Iron Pillars

If God has placed you in a situation that you find slightly uncomfortable, you should ask Him to make you into a bronze wall and an iron pillar (see Jer 1:18). Pray that He gives you some backbone. God is in need of hundreds, even thousands, of servants who do not retreat at the slightest opposition.

As you enter what God wants you to do and begin to feel a little resistance, do not run home and complain that everything is pointless and nothing seems to work. Instead, ask God to put something in you that will enable you to work under even the most unbearable conditions.

You may be afraid of being resisted to the extent that Jeremiah was. But never forget that there has probably never been another man with as much of God's glory over his life, or as much revelation, as Jeremiah.

The book of Jeremiah is full of revelation that reaches far into the New Covenant. He prophesied concerning the Messiah. He spoke about the New Covenant. He prophesied about a mighty outpouring of the Spirit and a whole host of other things for which God had given him revelation.

Just remember, if your path is a little difficult and trying, God will strengthen you so that you will manage to walk it. God will speak to you so that you are able to understand what He is saying, in spite of your circumstances. However, you must decide not to stray from the path.

You need to make up your mind not to give in when you meet with resistance or when the results seem a long time in coming. Decide not to back down in the face of any form of persecution. The Bible clearly says that if you are forced to suffer persecution, the Spirit of glory will rest upon you (1 Pet 4:14).

THE CALLING

15

Called!

Therefore, brethren, be even more diligent to make your calling and election sure, for if you do these things you will never stumble (2 Pet 1:10).

While this scripture is true for every believer, whatever his calling or ministry, it applies to the prophet in a special way. He will be presented with many opportunities to back down from his calling because of the fact that his work involves cleaning up the Body of Christ.

The prophet could be described as God's garbage collector. Unless a prophet has a consuming passion for purity, he is not a prophet; he is just a talker. The prophet's eager desire is to ensure that everything is clean, tidy and in order for the king's arrival. This is his ministry.

God reveals Himself in a powerful way so that the prophet can carry out his ministry through dreams, visions and revelations, which enable the prophet to see.

I once heard about a person who received a vision from heaven. He could see beautiful, green leaves and everything looked so nice. On closer inspection, however, he found that the underside of the leaves were covered with lice. This is the ministry of the prophet in a nutshell; he sees things that no one else sees.

The prophet's calling is also his problem. His unique gifting and ministry are also his anxiety. When he sees "lice," there may be others who do not want to see them, or who say, "Christians cannot have them!"

As a result, resistance arises which says, "We don't need any cleaning here. We'll just spray on a little paint and things will look just fine." As this opposition comes against the ministry of the prophet, he can let it affect him if he is not careful, and can find himself trying to get into line and look as nice and sweet as everyone else.

The prophet can become involved in church politics like anyone else, pat people on the back, shake their hands and smile pleasantly. But his calling is not merely to smile and pat people on the back or to look nice and ask them how they feel. He can do these things as an ordinary believer, but his ministry is to remove sin and uncleanness from the Church so that it is filled with a sweet fragrance, ready for Jesus' return.

Steadfast in the Calling

However, few people are willing to make these adjustments in their churches or personal lives, and because of this the prophet is often harshly attacked. He may be accused of being judgmental, hard and lacking in love. These accusations come automatically to anyone who is a prophet. While everyone else is saying that all is well, the prophet says the opposite. This often produces some sharp reactions.

At that point, the prophet must return to his calling—something we all need to do occasionally, no matter what our calling or anointing. He needs to make his election sure so he is not moved or tricked into either backing down from what he is to do or from doing more than he is supposed to do. Both will steal the prophet's strength and create problems, for himself and others.

Usually the prophet has a much stronger awareness of his calling than the other ministry gifts. However, this does not imply that to be truly called, every prophet must be commissioned in the same way as Isaiah.

In the year that King Uzziah died, I saw the Lord sitting on a throne, high and lifted up, and the train of His robe filled the temple. Above it stood seraphim; each one had six wings: with two he covered his face, with two he covered his feet, and with two he flew. And one cried to another and said: "Holy, holy, holy is the Lord of hosts; The whole earth is full of His glory!" (Isa 6:1-3)

God called Isaiah into the ministry through a powerful vision. The first aspect of God's character that Isaiah came in contact with was His holiness. Holiness is purity—and God is thorough when it comes to purity.

Of course, there can never be a perfect church. As soon as people are involved, there will be problems. None of us is able to live completely free from sin or problems, but God looks on the attitude of the heart.

A Time to Speak—A Time to be Quiet

While people may smile and look pleasant on the outside, inside they may bear hatred and great distress. The prophet sees these things, but he may not always be given permission to point them out. The prophet is not allowed to run around telling people all about their problems.

There are times when people are not at all open to correction because of stubbornness, hardness, pride or something else. The Spirit of God needs to work in their lives until they become humble enough to want to get rid of their problem and receive correction. Then God is able to send them people who will point out their problem, and show them the solution.

If you have no interest in helping people, God will never speak to you regarding the lives of others. Neither will God expose your secrets for every prophet who happens to pass by. He is a gentleman who does not reveal things or make them public indiscriminately. You can be secure in Him, knowing that He loves you and wants to help you. When this help comes, though, you must be open to receive it.

Dramatic Callings

And the posts of the door were shaken by the voice of him who cried out, and the house was filled with smoke.

So I said: "Woe is me, for I am undone! Because I am a man of unclean lips, and I dwell in the midst of a people of unclean lips; for my eyes have seen the King, the Lord of hosts." Then one of the seraphim flew to me, having in his hand a live coal which he had taken with the tongs from the altar. And he touched my mouth with it, and said: "Behold, this has touched your lips; your iniquity is taken away, and your sin purged." Also I heard the voice of the Lord, saying: "Whom shall I send, and who will go for Us?" Then I said, "Here am I! Send me." And He said, "Go, and tell this people: 'Keep on hearing, but do not understand; keep on seeing, but do not perceive.' Make the heart of this people dull, and their ears heavy, and shut their eyes; lest they see with their eyes, and hear with their ears, and understand with their heart, and return and be healed" (Isa 6:4-10).

Isaiah experienced an extremely dramatic calling. However, we know that God was later to place him in a very uncomfortable situation, and because of that he would need a strong awareness of his calling to fall back on.

Another person whom God placed in a difficult position was the prophet Ezekiel. He had an incredibly strong calling on his life. The entire first chapter of the book of Ezekiel contains a mighty revelation from God. He was shown a whirlwind and a great cloud with raging fire and the likeness of four living creatures. He saw the wheels and the throne and the brightness—he saw fantastic things.

Almost every dream and vision you could ever wish to have was shown to Ezekiel all at once. He looked directly into heaven and God spoke to him: *And He said to me, "Son of man, stand on your feet, and I will speak to you"* (Ezek 2:1).

All prophets who come into contact with the holiness and the nature of God fall prostrate and become weak in their natural selves. This is the Spirit of God at work, utterly destroying their natural strength.

Each of us comes to the point where we realize that without God, it is impossible to do what He has called us to do. We have all said this at one time or another and known it as a mental truth. "That's right, the Bible says that without God we can do nothing." However, it is one thing to agree mentally and yet continue to operate in soulish strength, and quite another to realize that events are headed for disaster without God.

When you realize this, you will become dependent on the presence and power of God, dying to your own strength and your own abilities.

There is sound teaching regarding living in the death of Christ. However, there is also a lot of wrong teaching in this area. For instance, as soon as you want to do something for God, some people will tell you that you have to die first. You are never quite "dead" enough to be able to do something for God.

We are not referring to this, at all. We are talking about being dependent on the Spirit of God, and we see this dependence when we enter God's presence:

Then the Spirit entered me when He spoke to me, and set me on my feet; and I heard Him who spoke to me. And He said to me: "Son of man, I am sending you to the children of Israel, to a rebellious nation that has rebelled against Me; they and their fathers have transgressed against Me to this very day. For they are impudent and stubborn children. I am sending you to them, and you shall say to them, 'Thus says the Lord God.' As for them, whether they hear or whether they refuse—for they are a rebellious house—yet they will know that a prophet has been among them. And you, son of man, do not be afraid of them nor be afraid of their words, though briers and thorns are with you and you dwell among scorpions; do not be afraid of their words or dismayed by their looks, though they are a rebellious house. You shall speak My words to them, whether they hear or whether they refuse, for they are rebellious. But you, son of man, hear what I say to you. Do not be rebellious like that rebellious house; open your mouth and eat what I give you." Now when I looked, there was a hand stretched out to me; and behold, a scroll of a book was in it. Then He spread it before me; and there was writing on the inside and on the outside, and written on it were lamentations and mourning and woe (Ezek 2:2-10).

What a calling! Just imagine—if these are Ezekiel's blessings, what would his curses look like? But all this concerns a specialist ministry. For example, if a North Sea oil rig explodes, it is not time to go looking for a carpenter. Someone is needed who can extinguish the fire, even if you have to search the world over to find them.

In the same way, the prophet has a specialist ministry that enables him to enter unique situations under undesirable conditions and do something of tremendous importance that will have a far-reaching effect; far beyond the place where he is currently working.

What an "encouragement" for Ezekiel: *"I am sending you to the children of Israel, those backslidden heathens, and your life will be less than enjoyable. You will dwell among snakes and scorpions, thorns and thistles. But don't listen to them! It will not help you to listen to them—it will only make you afraid. Instead, speak my word to them. By the way, they aren't going to listen to you, either. But whether or not they listen, they will know that a prophet has been in their midst. Make sure that you too are not rebellious, otherwise what is over them will also come over you. So pay attention and eat what I give you and then speak to them."*

It is Not Your Choice

This was the powerful calling of a prophet who was to do remarkable things and this was why the calling on his life was so strong. Ezekiel would be given thousands of opportunities to back down and compromise his call.

When Isaiah was called, he was made aware of his own uncleanness by coming into contact with the holiness of God. Therefore he preached *holiness,* even when he was sent to those who were disobedient.

When Ezekiel was called, he became aware of his own inability. He was given a glimpse into the spiritual realm and his calling from God came through powerful visions and revelations. In this way he would understand that God had all the ability that was necessary, even in the most unfavorable, unyielding, impossible and miserable situations imaginable.

This gave Ezekiel the ability to endure in the midst of a backslidden people. God placed him there, Ezekiel did exactly what he was meant to do, and the result was a great blessing for many people.

"Before I formed you in the womb I knew you; Before you were born I sanctified you; I ordained you a prophet to the nations." Then said I: "Ah, Lord God! Behold, I cannot speak, for I am a youth." But the Lord said to me: "Do not say, 'I am a youth,' For you shall go to all to whom I send you, And whatever I command you, you shall speak" (Jer 1:5-7).

This is the condition that God puts on each of His servants, especially on the prophet. You cannot make up your own mind about where to go or what to say. You must go where God sends you and say what He commands you.

You will see things that are not as they should be, particularly if there is a prophetic anointing on your life. In every situation, every church and every individual you are bound to find things that are wrong. When you discover this, your only response should be to pray.

If you see an individual behaving wrongly, usually the correct thing to do is to go to that person and speak with him yourself, rather than trying to get someone else to do it. If you feel that you should not do this, then you should pray—and keep your lips sealed.

If you have something from God, you never need to explain or defend it. Your only task is to deliver it. After this you are released. You have nothing more to do; you need only obey God.

It is important to be obedient when the word comes. So be firmly established in the calling God has given you, whatever your ministry gift may be. When God has given you a word to deliver, you must be obedient. When you are, God will protect you, take care of you and defend you, and the word you bring will bear much fruit.

THE PROPHET'S WEAKNESSES

16

Isolation

In the New Testament, the prophets often worked together in a group. This is a tremendous blessing for them, because one of the greatest attacks launched against the prophet is that of isolation. The prophet carries a message that is highly unconventional. He can see a little farther and a little more than people in general, and this is not always appreciated. As a result, he can begin to feel sorry for himself, become exhausted and isolate himself.

Everyone has an inner desire to be appreciated by others. There is nothing wrong with this. The Bible tells us to honor one another above ourselves (Rom 12:10 NIV). Therefore, it is not wrong to give someone a compliment or show other expressions of appreciation. We are meant to do this.

However, your flesh often wants to do exactly the opposite; to find fault, criticize and complain. But God has something higher than this for us. He wants us to bless and honor one another. It is always easier for us when people like what we do, rather than when they do not approve of it. It obviously feels nicer when they send flowers instead of throwing eggs!

Nonetheless, it is vital that the prophet in particular is free from other people's opinions. The person who enters a prophetic office must be free from rejection. A person with deep-seated rejection and a difficult, problematic background, who has always had people against him, can get the idea that he is automatically qualified to be a prophet. However, this merely creates a type of persecution complex about the wrong things.

An Attempt to Protect Oneself

The prophet often responds with isolation in order to protect himself. He needs solitude and he enjoys taking time to be alone with God. However, this can become his lifestyle as he isolates himself from others for fear that they will reject him.

Preaching requires a tremendous amount of mental energy. I am not referring to seven minutes of meditation, but to a proper meeting. There is often resistance in the spirit realm and it is necessary to draw on every available bit of physical and mental energy. Afterwards you can be quite exhausted.

The enemy usually comes at this point. The parasites and critics begin to show up. It is easy to be slightly more sensitive and weak after having preached. The enemy knows this, and so this is when he strikes.

Such was the case with Elijah. He had just cut off the heads of 450 prophets of Baal and had seen the fire fall on Mount Carmel. But Jezebel only needed to open her mouth and say, "You will die in the same way as those prophets, Elijah. Wherever you are, I'm going to find you" (see 1 Kings 19:2).

After being so bold before 450 men, Elijah now trembled before a woman. However, she was not just any woman; a spirit of death had been released through her against Elijah's prophetic anointing. He ran away and hid, went into isolation and wished he were dead.

Such isolation is an unhealthy, personal choice and you must beware of this, especially if you stand in the office of a prophet.

17

Exclusivity

God does not want the prophet to think that he is somehow exclusive. This is dangerous enough, but along with exclusivity comes pride, contempt and criticism. God does not want you to have these things in your life.

If you do have a prophetic anointing, you will see things that others do not see. While others have the impression that all is well, you may be seeing areas that are seriously wrong. Then, if you are not careful, your flesh will cultivate a critical disposition or a general attitude of contempt toward others.

There is a danger that the prophet may think more highly of himself than he ought. He is just a messenger, or a divine mailman, not someone who wraps himself in a prophetic mantle and walks around feeling special and unique. Such an attitude is wrong. He may be a carpenter, an unskilled worker or a lumberjack. He is just a normal person who happens to have a prophetic anointing on his life.

If you stand in a prophetic ministry, you must not develop an exclusive attitude, as this may lead you to dangerously believe that no one ever understands you. The prophet has a strong awareness of his calling, so he can become very "self-centered" if he is not careful. Therefore, it is important that he lives a normal life, fellowships with ordinary people and does something useful with his hands.

This will protect him from becoming introspective and thinking that no one is able to understand him.

"The Prophetic Freedom"

If you are a prophet and you consider yourself too good to witness, then you are a backslidden prophet. If you never get involved in the everyday needs of others, there is something suspect about you. You need to break the exclusivity and isolation that surrounds you so you can take part in the normal activities of the church.

You have no right to come and go as you please and do whatever suits you all the time. "The prophetic freedom" can easily pull people into the flesh and make them think they have the right to do whatever they want. These people can sometimes be extremely undisciplined, constantly using their high and mighty revelations to excuse themselves.

However, despite the number of great revelations, prophets still have to eat a normal daily diet. They need to live a normal life and take responsibility in the natural, and not just "space-out" on every imaginable form of "revelation."

You need to get rid of vanity, exclusivity, isolationist tendencies, pride and contempt, or you will begin to belittle those whom you feel do not understand things as well as you. The devil will tell you, "No one else has such a strong prophetic anointing as you. You really see what goes on in the spirit world." In this way a contempt for others is created and exclusivity begins to emerge.

If you listen to the wrong voice you will become vain, exclusive and proud. You will become isolated and disdain others, and the devil will be able to break you. However, if you guard against such tendencies these things will not happen.

18

Perfectionism

One of the prophet's most typical weaknesses is that of exaggerated perfectionism. When everyone else is full of joy after a wonderful meeting in which great things have happened, the prophet says, "Yes, but it could have been better." This is typical "prophet-flesh!"

Of course, there has never been a meeting where there could not have been even more of the glory of God. However, such a negative attitude which completely overlooks the good that took place, and concentrates on one minor negative detail, is not from heaven.

The prophet is subject to numerous attacks mainly because he is more sensitive than others to what is taking place in the spirit world. He perceives things which others do not. This is generally true for anyone in a position of responsibility. They are like the pillars that hold up the ceiling; they bear the weight, while those who sit underneath the ceiling feel no pressure at all.

People who carry responsibility, stand and hold things up, which means they feel the weight and the resistance that others do not experience. However, do not begin to complain about how heavy things are and about the resistance you feel in the meeting. You should mention this only if the Holy Spirit is telling the congregation to pray about them.

The person who holds a prophetic office—or some other position of responsibility—must learn to correctly interpret his experiences and impressions. Unless he learns to live with the gift of discerning of spirits, which is exactly what we are talking about here, this gift can become too much for him to bear.

The prophet has a "narrow field of ministry." He can be compared with the eye surgeon who, like the heart surgeon, is extremely specialized. Both are well aware of their special fields. The prophet is similar. Therefore he must resist pride and perfectionism so that he can accept the fact that events do not always happen exactly as he would like them to.

An apostle can often be influential and preach with power, but in his approach to life, details mean very little. He may sleep on a sofa and get up the next day to travel to the mission field. But not the prophet! Little things can easily disturb him. He likes to have everything in order when he flows in his ministerial anointing. This is an element of his ministry. The music must be right, for instance, and he can be disturbed by things that are out of place.

This can carry over into the natural so that he develops a lifestyle of being overly fussy. If others do not preach exactly what he wants to hear, or exactly what he thinks is right for the moment, he sits there getting upset. The message failed to tickle his ears. The fact that thousands of others were helped does not matter. He considers only himself and what he is experiencing at the present moment. He needs to rid himself of this mind-set and instead begin to pay attention to those around him.

He may even say, "No, I don't feel like praying for people right now. There is no anointing present!" But we can pray for people at any time. There may indeed be a special anointing when one really *must* pray for people, but irrespective of this, one can always pray for others.

Jonah—Critical, Complaining and Self-centered

When God told Jonah, "Go to Nineveh," he went in a completely different direction rather than do what God had told him to do. Then, after being more or less forced to obey, he became upset, complaining and critical. Jonah is an excellent example of a troublesome prophet in the Old Testament. God was forced to keep pushing him. He ended up in the belly of the whale and not until his circumstances became unbearable did he finally obey—and even this was merely outward obedience.

Jonah finally went to Nineveh and delivered the message of warning and judgment that God had given him. Then he sat down outside the city and waited for God to judge them, although to his great disappointment the Ninevites paid attention to the message from heaven and repented.

"What is this all about?" thought Jonah. "God was supposed to judge the city! This is embarrassing for me!"

The entire city had repented, but Jonah sat under a bush and wished he were dead. He was critical, complaining and self-centered. He thought only about himself. The plant that God had caused to grow to provide Jonah with shade had withered and Jonah felt miserable.

Finally God grew tired of Jonah and said, *You have had pity on the plant for which you have not labored, nor made it grow, which came up in a night and perished in a night. And should I not pity Nineveh, that great city, in which are more than one hundred and twenty thousand persons who cannot discern between their right hand and their left—and much livestock?* (Jon 4:10-11) God even had compassion on their livestock!

Many people are just like Jonah. They say, "Oh, I have such a calling. God has given me such a burden." But God never places a heavy burden on you; not if you are obedient, that is. However, some people do nothing but complain. They are obstinate, self-centered and egotistical.

This kind of person may say, "No one understands me; if only you knew how it feels. You'd better believe that *I* had to work for this. I had to go through a lot to get it." A response of this nature is merely embarrassing for both yourself and even for God.

God does not call people to be frustrated; He calls them to work. When God employs you, He gives you something to do with your hands.

If your calling is that of a prophet, you have been called for the sake of other people! However, no one has a greater tendency than the prophet to become introspective and to forget the purpose of his calling. He brings exclusivity and isolation on himself because of his own frustration, due to his own disobedience.

Knowing this, we can understand that the most frustrated person to be found in the Old Testament was Jonah, who was consistently disobedient. Even when he obeyed God he was being disobedient.

Jeremiah—The Persecuted One

Jeremiah, however, was quite different from Jonah. As a prophet he was of a much nobler character, although he received so much persecution that he wished he had never been born (Jer 20:14).

Then I said, "I will not make mention of Him, Nor speak any more in His name." But His word was in my heart like a burning fire Shut up in my bones; I was weary of holding it back, And I could not (Jer 20:9).

God told Jeremiah, *If you return, Then I will bring you back; You shall stand before me; If you take out the precious from the vile, You shall be as My mouth* (Jer 15:19).

Every one of God's prophets has, at some time, resisted his calling. Their calling was not always a bed of roses. Their lives involved more than just apparent successes. Even Moses went so far as to ask God to deliver him from the rebellious people whom he could no longer bear (Num 11:10-15).

The prophets of the Old Testament had a unique calling that involved cleansing, restoration, establishment, foundation and direction among a people who were often completely uninterested in listening to what they had to say. They were therefore forced to be established in their callings, rather than in their personalities. When they stood and spoke on the Lord's behalf but no one listened to them, it was vital that they were completely free from rejection.

19

Compromise

And the word of the Lord came to Elijah the Tishbite, saying, "See how Ahab has humbled himself before Me? Because he has humbled himself before Me, I will not bring the calamity in his days. In the days of his son I will bring the calamity on his house." Now three years passed without war between Syria and Israel. Then it came to pass, in the third year, that Jehoshaphat the king of Judah went down to visit the king of Israel. And the king of Israel said to his servants, "Do you know that Ramoth in Gilead is ours, but we hesitate to take it out of the hand of the king of Syria?" So he said to Jehoshaphat, "Will you go with me to fight at Ramoth Gilead?" Jehoshaphat said to the king of Israel, "I am as you are, my people as your people, my horses as your horses (1 Kings 21:28-22:4).

Every king has an inner desire to conquer. This desire is also present in us, as new creations, because of the godly inheritance and nature we have received. We have the desire to expand and increase. This is a part of us as a royal priesthood (1 Pet 2:9; Rev 1:6). We rule and reign together with Christ Jesus.

Jehoshaphat had this desire to conquer and that is why he immediately supported the suggestion from the king of Israel. But then he remembered that they might need a confirmation from the Lord before setting out:

Also Jehoshaphat said to the king of Israel, "Please inquire for the word of the Lord today." Then the king of Israel gathered the prophets together, about four hundred men, and said to them, "Shall I go against Ramoth Gilead to fight, or shall I refrain? So they said, "Go up, for the Lord will deliver it into the hand of the king." And Jehoshaphat said, "Is there not still a prophet of the Lord here, that we may inquire of him?" So the king of Israel said to Jehoshaphat, "There is still one man, Micaiah the son of Imlah, by whom we may inquire of the Lord; but I hate him, because he does not prophesy good concerning me, but evil." And Jehoshaphat said, "Let not the king say such things!" Then the king of Israel called an officer and said, "Bring Micaiah the son of Imlah quickly!" The king of Israel and Jehoshaphat the king of Judah, having put on their robes, sat each on his throne, at a threshing floor at the entrance of the gate of Samaria; and all the prophets prophesied before them. Now Zedekiah the son of Chenaanah had made horns of iron for himself; and he said, "Thus says the Lord: 'With these you shall gore the Syrians until they are destroyed.' " And all the prophets prophesied so, saying, "Go up to Ramoth Gilead and prosper, for the Lord will deliver it into the king's hand." Then the messenger who had gone to call Micaiah spoke to him, saying, "Now listen, the words of the prophets with one accord encourage the king. Please, let your word be like the word of one of them, and speak encouragement"

(1 Kings 22:5-13).

God's General Will

There is something very wrong when everyone is always saying the same thing. In this case, such people are not real prophets, they are merely parrots. But Ahab was delighted. Success, prosperity and happiness—he thought this sounded wonderful.

"Hallelujah," he said. "That's what I like to hear. They're really flowing in the anointing now!" The prophecy he heard suited him perfectly. But Jehoshaphat was slightly more spiritual and thought that Ahab was a bit too happy for his own good.

What a sight! There sat the two kings dressed in their royal attire while 400 prophets crowed like roosters and prophesied exactly what the kings wanted to hear. If all you ever do is prophesy what other people want to hear, then you are not a prophet; you are nothing but an ear-tickler.

The general will of God, of course, is success and victory and these prophets were prophesying just this. For example, it is His general will to heal everyone. However, unless the conditions for God's will are fulfilled in the life of a particular individual, you cannot prophesy specifically that this person will be healed. Otherwise you would have spoken a false prophecy, even though it may be in line with God's general will.

God's general will for the king was obviously success, but because he did not live in obedience, there was no foundation on which success could become a reality in his life. Therefore these prophecies offered only false comfort and whitewashed the real issues. You cannot offer people cheap grace. Only when they have made a heartfelt repentance, renounced sin and submitted to God is there a basis for prophesying grace and success. Ahab's 400 prophets brought nothing but good wishes.

However, Jehoshaphat was not satisfied until one more prophet was called. So a messenger was sent to Micaiah, saying, "Now listen here, Micaiah, you have been given a very special task. You are being asked to come before the king. Be wise, now, Micaiah! Don't be foolish, just take it easy—for two reasons."

"First of all, you must not disturb the king. It would be terrible if something got stirred up. Secondly, you need to think about your career. Arrange the words neatly, pat them on the back and shake a few hands. Give them a friendly wink. Just say something general and nice, something about the fact that God loves them."

And Micaiah said, "As the Lord lives, whatever the Lord says to me, that I will speak" (1 Kings 22:14).

For the Truth

There was not an ounce of compromise in Micaiah. *Compromise presents the greatest danger for the prophet.* As soon as he begins to compromise, his entire ministry falls apart. He begins to speak based on personal imaginations that can cause great damage and bring a curse on the Body of Christ.

The prophet must never compromise. His ministry depends on it. No one is supposed to compromise, but the consequences of a prophet compromising are particularly serious.

Then he came to the king; and the king said to him, "Micaiah, shall we go to war against Ramoth Gilead, or shall we refrain?" And he answered him, "Go and prosper, for the Lord will deliver it into the hand of the king!" So the king said to him, "How many times shall I make you swear that you tell me nothing but the truth in the name of the Lord?" The king knew that Micaiah was withholding the truth. Then he said, "I saw all Israel scattered on the mountains, as sheep that have no shepherd. And the Lord said, 'These have no master. Let each return to his own house in peace'. "And the king of Israel said to Jehoshaphat, "Did I not tell you that he would not prophesy good concerning me, but evil?" (1 Kings 22:15-18)

King Ahab was not interested in hearing the truth; he only wanted to get his project approved.

Then Micaiah said, "Therefore hear the word of the Lord: I saw the Lord sitting on His throne, and all the host of heaven standing by, on His right hand and on His left. And the Lord said, 'Who will persuade Ahab to go up, that he may fall at Ramoth Gilead?' So one spoke in this manner, and another spoke in that manner. Then a spirit came forward and stood before the Lord, and said, 'I will persuade him.' The Lord said to him, 'In what way?' So he said, 'I will go out and be a lying spirit in the mouth of all his prophets.' And the Lord said, 'You shall persuade him, and also prevail. Go out and do so.' " "Therefore, look! The Lord has put a lying spirit in the mouth of all these prophets of yours, and the Lord has declared disaster against you." Then Zedekiah the son of Chenaanah went near and struck Micaiah on the cheek, and said, "Which way did the spirit from the Lord go from me to speak to you?" And Micaiah said, "Indeed, you shall see on that day when you go into an inner chamber to hide!" Then the king of Israel said, "Take Micaiah, and return him to Amon the governor of the city and to Joash the king's son; and say, 'Thus says the king: Put this fellow in prison, and feed him with bread of affliction and water of affliction, until I come in peace.' " Then Micaiah said, "If you ever return in peace, the Lord has not spoken by me." And he said, "Take heed, all you people!" (1 Kings 22:19-28)

What Micaiah said was, "Remember this: if the king returns then I am a false prophet. But I want you to know this one thing, the king will not return." And neither did the king return.

This is a prophet. Micaiah had more than enough opportunities to compromise, but instead he said, "I can't do it. I can't do anything other than what the Lord tells me to do. In fact, what the Lord tells me is right and what He tells them is a lie."

Some may ask, "Who do you think you are to imagine that you alone have the truth and all others are wrong? What makes you so special?" If the prophet tries to make himself something special, he will only end up acting exclusively and belittling everyone. However, God prophets are indeed special, when they speak what He tells them to speak. They are not exclusive, it is the Word that comes through them. It is possible for one person to be right and for everyone else to be wrong.

There once was a man of God named Martin Luther. He was right in his views while the rest of Christianity at that time was wrong. He was right and everyone else was wrong. Because he stood up for the truth, Christianity was turned in the right direction.

We can thank God today that he refused to compromise by saying, "Well, we are only human. We all make mistakes, but there is a point in what I'm saying. Why don't you assess what I've discovered and see if there's anything there that might be of some worth to you? Perhaps you can use it in one of your devotionals."

Micaiah said, "This is true. You will not return. If you do return, then I am not a true prophet." A person who is this bold knows what he is talking about. He is speaking the prophetic word.

Of course, Micaiah was thrown into prison. This usually happens to a prophet! However, it was better to be right and be in prison than to sit at the king's table and prophesy good wishes.

It was embarrassing for Zedekiah and the other prophets when the king did actually die on the battlefield. Their only defence was to quickly come up with an explanation like, "God is beyond our understanding and He can change His mind. We will never fully understand His ways," or to invent a similar form of theology, to protect themselves.

20

Super-spirituality

A prophet does not always take a systematic approach to teaching and preaching. He may jump back and forth as he preaches under prophetic inspiration. He sees different things, and this can express itself in a variety of ways.

Therefore, the teacher is a great help to the prophet, and they often work together. The prophet needs the clear-sightedness of the teacher to help him avoid digressions and allowing his imagination to run wild. His revelations must be in accordance with the scriptures.

Something about the prophetic anointing causes the prophet to suddenly see symbols in scripture, no matter what the context. He flows in the gift of revelation, and if he should get out into the flesh, he starts to crave a little more revelation. He wants something that is unique only to him.

God told some of His prophets to do some very extraordinary things. He told Jeremiah, for instance, to buy a linen sash and wear it around his waist. After that, he was instructed to hide it in a hole in the rock. A long time later, God told Jeremiah to go and get the sash, which he discovered completely ruined. Based on these actions, God drew a parallel with the people of Israel (see Jer 13). God used this prophetic deed to convey a truth.

Prophetic deeds sometimes involve music and dance, but this must be prompted by the Holy Spirit. Someone may suggest having a prophetic dance or a prophetic parade, but such ideas are not necessarily from God.

There is always a risk of becoming super-spiritual regarding the prophetic anointing. This is why it is important for prophets to stay in touch with other ministers. If they let themselves be drawn away by their feelings they can easily invent some strange and sensationalistic prophetic deeds.

They can also over interpret the scriptures by seeing all kinds of connections that are hidden to everyone else. This is a real danger and can create contempt for the prophetic office. Therefore God must cleanse this area so that the prophetic area retains its heavenly power and reputation.

Be Normal!

If you are entering a prophetic ministry, or have a prophetic anointing on your life, it is vital that you do not compromise, surround yourself with exclusivity, indulge in self-pity, or become proud or critical. Instead, you should draw the anointing and the joy of God over your life. If you keep your personal life normal, God will be able to increase your prophetic anointing and make you a great blessing to others. Then when you get a word from God, you will be free and pure and able to deliver that word. As a result, the lives of thousands of people will be changed.

In other words, simply having a calling to be a prophet is not sufficient. You must also attend to your personal life, as you will be equated with the message you bring. You cannot develop bizarre tendencies and traits as some prophets do. You must continue to function in the ministry of the ordinary believer, continue to be spontaneous with others and live a normal life simultaneous with your ministry.

If you do this, the prophetic anointing will increase. If you are careful not to develop these negative characteristics, but continue as a normal believer, God will be able to use you powerfully. God needs thousands of prophets who can hear from Him and say, "This is what the Lord is saying right now."

WORDS FROM HEAVEN CAN CHANGE NATIONS

21

The Country Can Be Changed!

Do not think in your heart that you will escape in the king's palace any more than all the other Jews. For if you remain completely silent at this time, relief and deliverance will arise for the Jews from another place, but you and your father's house will perish. Yet who knows whether you have come to the kingdom for such a time as this? (Esth 4:13-14)

When Esther became queen, she received the favor of the king, and was thus able to speak prophetically to him and consequently save her people. However, she was tempted to remain quiet and take no action, hoping to stay secluded and secure in the royal palace. But God sent her a message to encourage and strengthen her to bold action.

Mordecai warned Esther not to compromise in this situation. He said, "If you think you will survive simply because you live in the king's house, you will be disappointed. They will take you as well. But if you are bold and realize that you have attained a royal position for a purpose, which is to save your people, and if you act on the calling and anointing that you have received in this position, then you will have success and your people will be saved."

A People With the Spirit and Power of Elijah

Esther is a picture both of the Church and an ordinary believer. God has not placed us in our country just to be generally nice and to say pleasant things, but in order to speak out what the Spirit of God is saying to the nation, or even to another nation.

We need to believe that God can use us to save our country from all the misery in it. There is salvation for every situation and for every person. If we believe that as a church we should be concerned only with ourselves, we have missed God's intention for us.

We have been called by God for a time such as this. We have been created to live in this day and age. We are not like those who lived in the sixteen, seventeen or eighteen hundreds. We are different, and by the grace of God, we are who we are. The time in which we live is also different. We are living in very special days.

Just as God raised up John the Baptist to prepare for Jesus' arrival here on earth, He is raising up today a whole generation with the spirit and power of Elijah over their lives. He is not raising up a new Elijah, but a people with his anointing; an anointing of confrontation, preparation and reformation in order to prepare for the return of Jesus.

However, first some spring cleaning is required. We must put things in order so the Lord can come again. This is our calling. If you believe this and praise God for it, you will see these things happen before your very eyes.

God will change this nation. Its people must be saved and the Church must be strengthened, and you can be among those whom God will use to do it. He will not use just one person to do all this; He will raise up many. His people, His prophetic church, will be used to speak, particularly to the government. Government ministers who stand and spew out lies and ungodly speech will feel their knees begin to shake.

In Ezekiel 7:11, the Bible says, *Violence has risen up into a rod of wickedness.* This is exactly the situation in many of our countries today. However, we have the ability to pray against this and see our country changed. We can watch revival come and see righteousness return once again.

The office of the prophet is one part of this process. His ministry is necessary in bringing about the change we desire. For many of us, prophetic visions and messages have not been common occurrences. They have taken place in small prayer groups and hidden nooks and crannies. But Jeremiah was not such a prophet. He did not retreat to a basement and mumble a few words. He spoke publicly for everyone to hear.

A time is coming when the Church must stop writing its articles of faith and begin prophesying instead. We need to stop simply making a "contribution to the debate" and start speaking the earthshattering Word of the Lord. Our words should contain such power that they shake the nation, right up to the governmental offices.

One Single Purpose

Then the Lord put forth His hand and touched my mouth, and the Lord said to me: "Behold, I have put my words in your mouth. See, I have this day set you over the nations and over the kingdoms, To root out and to pull down, To destroy and to throw down, To build and to plant" (Jer 1:9-10).

Here we see four "negative" words and two "positive" words. First there is rooting out, pulling down, destroying and throwing down, then building up and planting. Many would like to skip over the first part of the verse and what it implies, preferring the idea of building up and planting instead, because it sounds so positive.

We are positive and preach a positive Gospel, but we are not so "positive" that we tell people that the devil does not exist. We know that there is an enemy who *walks about like a roaring lion, seeking whom he may devour* (1 Pet 5:8), and we resist him, steadfast in the faith, knowing that he must flee from us.

We walk in victory and trample on snakes and scorpions and over all the power of the enemy, and nothing shall by any means harm us (Luke 10:19). We speak the Word of God, in faith, against the devil and he is forced to flee from us (Jas 4:7). We take up the shield of faith that extinguishes all the fiery darts of Satan (Eph 6:16).

We are aware of the total situation and therefore, we need not concentrate only on the negative. We do not focus only on the hindrances in our path, nor on the path itself, nor only on the goal set before us. We see every aspect.

We speak what the Holy Spirit gives us to say in a particular situation, whether it has to do with the hindrances, the path or the ultimate goal. We speak out whatever the Lord places in our mouths, whether it is to build up and plant, or to root up and destroy. *Everything has one and the same purpose: to prepare for the Lord a people who are pleasing to Him and prepared for His return.* This is the overall, general purpose.

Of course, the enemy does not like this. He would rather see a church, even one with ten thousand members, where everyone is in rebellion, has problems with sin and where a great amount of demonic influence and worldliness abound. Such an army is useless.

This is why God works with the Church and society simultaneously. He cleanses, restores and disciplines the Body of Christ to make us what He desires, and to give us a strong influence on every level and in every place the Holy Spirit leads us. We will then be able to break down the demonic strongholds that stand in the way of people's salvation. Then we will see what God is longing for: a revival in the land.

Many people say, "Elijah prayed that it wouldn't rain, and for three and a half years there was not a drop of it. Then He prayed that it would rain, and sure enough it did.

So let's pray for rain. Let's pray for the latter rain to fall." But have you ever thought about what happened before the rain could come? Elijah confronted Ahab and was on Mount Carmel where he cut off the heads of 450 prophets of Baal. There was a lot of work to be done before he could pray for the rain. Then when he prayed, the rain fell.

Sometimes we cry out and pray for revival. "Quickly, quickly, give us a little latter rain right now," we say. But in fact there are many things that need to be done in the spirit world before the Holy Spirit can come in power over His people and bring salvation to the world. The ministry of the prophet plays a vital role in this preparation and so you should not get angry or irritated with it. Rather than resisting it, you should receive the prophetic word, test whether or not it is from God, then humble yourself and submit to it.

The Prophet Belongs in the Church

As we know, the prophet has a church-building function. He serves the church with guidance, instruction, exhortation, judgment and revelation. This is actually what Jeremiah was told he would be doing in Jeremiah 1:10. Rooting out, pulling down, destroying, throwing down, building and planting are all aspects of putting the church in proper order.

Now in the church that was at Antioch there were certain prophets and teachers: Barnabas, Simeon who was called Niger, Lucius of Cyrene, Manaen who had been brought up with Herod the tetrarch, and Saul (Acts 13:1).

The natural setting for the prophet is the church. He is to work in the church providing guidance and direction, helping people, offering instruction, exhortation, various kinds of revelations, and bringing warning and judgment. He cooperates in the local church with the other ministry gifts that are there. He also travels out from the local church.

We often imagine the prophet as a lonely, isolated character, but in the New Testament they are almost always mentioned in the plural. There were many prophets. They were clearly able to agree in some way and to coordinate their various styles and ministries.

And in these days prophets came from Jerusalem to Antioch. Then one of them, named Agabus, stood up and showed by the Spirit that there was going to be a great famine throughout all the world, which also happened in the days of Claudius Caesar (Acts 11:27-28).

This prophesy was fulfilled. However, it would not surprise me if someone in the church at Antioch had stood up after Agabus had prophesied and said, "No, we pray against that! We confess that this famine will not come!" However, the Bible says that the famine "also happened!" When a prophetic message of this nature comes, you cannot merely say, "I am redeemed from famine!" because the message is from God.

God Has the Strategy

We can read of a prophet in the Old Testament called Elisha. When the king of Syria planned to attack Israel, Elisha sent a messenger to the king of Israel to tell him, "They are coming from over there. Put some troops there and attack them." And this is exactly what they did.

Finally, the king of Syria became completely frustrated. *He called his servants and said to them, "Will you not show me which of us is for the king of Israel?" And one of his servants said, "None, my lord, O king; but Elisha, the prophet who is in Israel, tells the king of Israel the words that you speak in your bedroom"* (2 Kings 6:11-12).

God is well aware of what will happen during the coming days. He also knows exactly where the attacks will come from. David always took the ephod and asked of the Lord, "What shall I do, God? From where will the attacks come?" and the Lord would reply and instruct him.

In the same way, the Holy Spirit will reveal to His prophets any approaching danger. If we learn to appreciate the prophetic word, the Holy Spirit can then tell us what will happen in our home town in the coming year, and how the church should respond to be able to meet what lies ahead.

22

The Lord Speaks to the Nation

God appoints prophets to cleanse, prepare and perfect the Church so that it matures into perfection. This is the task of all of the ministry gifts.

God also commissions prophets to preach prophetically and to reach even the disobedient, bringing them to repentance. They should also preach and prophesy regarding what will happen to different nations or individuals, so that both may come into the will of God.

Jeremiah was such a prophet. In Jeremiah 22:29 he prophesies, *O land, land, land, hear the word of the Lord!* (NIV).

Some prophetic messages will go out, not just to prayer groups or churches, but to entire nations. The prophetic ministry, both in the Old Testament and the present day, is not just limited to operating within the Church. It is a ministry with the unique function of establishing the Church, just as the temple was built through the prophets, but it also stretches far beyond this.

Right now, we will witness a restoration of the office of the prophet as never before. God is very careful regarding what is prophesied, because *the only thing that will change certain situations is to prophesy to or against the governmental authorities.* There are times when God's word regarding certain situations within a country must be proclaimed publicly.

The correct message can be given in the wrong spirit, which will cause it to lack any power of penetration. It is also possible to say the right thing, but too soon or in the wrong situation, and so fail to achieve any real breakthrough. However, if you have the *right word* to say, which is the unique ministry of the prophet, *at the right time to the right person in the right situation,* you will experience a *real breakthrough.*

God wants His Word to have great penetration and to break through in this country, both through the ministry of the prophet and the rest of His servants—ordinary believers and ministers alike. There is no reason for our country not to hear the Word of the Lord. There is no reason why our government should fail to seriously hear what God has to say. This applies not only to special proclamations of judgment on certain issues, but to everything that is covered in the Word of God. These words can come through the office of the prophet.

We Are Not Ashamed of Jesus!

Daniel had a strong prophetic ministry, which was severely tested. However, Daniel stood firm throughout the trials and achieved great victory. In this way, his prophetic ministry had a far-reaching effect on the entire city of Babylon.

After Shadrach, Meshach, Abednego and Daniel had withstood their trials, the whole country repented and the king proclaimed and decreed that their God was to be worshiped.

It is high time that this was proclaimed in all of our countries. People must see that our God is in control. This is why God is not busy raising up academics who sit around debating all the time: "On the one hand, on the other hand; on the one hand, on the other hand." Instead, He is raising up people—not just one or two, but many people and in a variety of ways—who speak out clearly and declare, "Thus says the Lord!"

Our countries need to hear the Word of the Lord. Many of them have not properly heard it yet. The Word of the Lord has not always been delivered from our pulpits, but instead rather watered-down versions of the Gospel, which have virtually apologized for what God has done for us. Quite simply, we have been ashamed of Jesus.

But a time has come when many people who are not at all ashamed of Jesus are rising up. We are not ashamed of Jesus when He heals the sick, nor are we ashamed of Him when He casts out demons. We are not ashamed of Jesus when He speaks His Word, knowing that this Word restores entire countries and brings great blessing to whole nations.

God first uses the prophetic ministry to encourage believers not to be ashamed, but, rather, to repent and become seriously committed to the Lord. He then uses the prophetic word to build us up and make us stronger and bolder so that we enter our proper function in the Body of Christ. Afterwards, we are able to prophesy beyond the walls of the church so that the Word of God strikes people in the society around us, from the highest to the lowest. As a result, God will then be able to change a great deal in our nation.

Battering Rams for the Lord

This was Jeremiah's function; to prophesy over nations and peoples. When he said, *O land, land, land, hear the word of the Lord!* he was not addressing just a few individual religious leaders. Instead, all the people heard what the Lord had to say.

In the same way, God will raise up preachers and public speakers in our countries. These people will not necessarily be polished or elegant. Neither will they engage in diplomatic discussions on television debate programs. But, they will cause things to shake, when they open their mouths. People will hear what they have to say and things will be changed.

During the days of Jeremiah, the nation was terribly backslidden. This is why God needed Jeremiah. Similarly, during the miserable circumstances of the Middle Ages, God needed a man like Luther. Things had to be shaken and changed.

If you read about the people God has used throughout church history, you will notice that they were not the kind of people who sat at home twiddling their thumbs, apologizing for their opinions. Instead, they were men and women who rose up in the power of the Holy Spirit and acted as battering rams for the Lord.

What our countries need—and what the whole world needs, for that matter—are battering rams for the Lord; people who are filled with the glory and the love of God and carrying the favor of men, yet aggressive enough to break through.

The greater the level of backsliding, the more powerful the prophetic ministry must be. The more stiff-necked the people are, the stronger the prophetic anointing that is required. God gives every man his due. This is the way He has always been and will always be. Therefore, He well knows which tool to use to get the job finished.

23

Treachery Toward the Nation

While I was studying to be a priest in Uppsala, Sweden, one of the professors invited a number of homosexuals— "Christian" homosexuals, as they referred to themselves— to one of our classes. They were asked to talk about the positive aspects of homosexuality to a group of between 200-300 prospective priests.

A small group of us knew that they were coming, so we took some time that morning to pray. We took authority over the spiritual forces that lie behind homosexuality (see Rom 1:26-27; Lev 18:22).

In reality, this part of our education was nothing more than the seduction of future priests to accept homosexuality as a genuine form of love. It was then hoped that they would go on to spread that opinion in churches throughout the country.

However, homosexuality is not a genuine display or expression of love. According to the Bible, it is an abomination in the eyes of God. Of course, just as with every other abomination, it is possible to be delivered from homosexuality. The blood of Jesus cleanses from *all* sin, when that sin is confessed. If evil spirits are involved, they can be cast out and the person can be set free.

The moment I set foot in the classroom that day, I noticed that for some reason the professor looked slightly shaken. He was upset and grumpy. It was obvious that the

which we had bound through our prayers,
urbed.

five homosexuals began to talk about how
was to be a homosexual and just how
...... Afterwards we had the opportunity to ask
questions. I could feel myself boiling inside, so I asked the
Lord, "Should I say something now?"

"No," He replied.

Someone stood up to say something that was basically
correct, but which seemed to be said at the wrong time and
therefore dropped to the ground like a dry leaf. They were
the right words, but said at the wrong time, and it was
obvious that they had no effect.

Then another man stood up and said something
generally apologetic about how hard and dogmatic
Christians had been and how we really should be more
understanding and loving. They were the wrong words at
the wrong time.

I sat praying quietly in tongues the whole time. Then I
asked the Lord, "Should I say something now?"

"No," He said. "You need to calm down a little bit." So I
just sat and waited.

"Should I say something now?" I asked.

"No!" He said.

"Now?" I asked.

"Yes!" He finally responded, "I want you to say it now."
Then I stood to my feet and put up my hand.

Right Words, Right Time

I was given the floor, so I turned to the first chapter of
Romans and read what it says there about homosexuality.
Then I said, "You say that homosexuality is talked about
only in the Old Testament and that the New Testament has
nothing to say about it, but rather just seems to accept it.
However, here in Romans 1:27 is the same word that is

used in Leviticus 18:22; the word "abomination." The Word of God says that homosexuality is not at all acceptable, but that it is an abomination."

I did not raise my voice or shout or prophesy; I just spoke calmly, lead by the Holy Spirit. However, when I said this, the entire auditorium exploded. The Word of God came into the room like a hammer. The otherwise cultivated, aesthetic, humane, humanistic professor had suddenly become a different man. What was really inside him suddenly came out; he became angry and irritated.

Someone else began to speak and I felt God telling me to request the right to reply. It was a panel discussion, so I said, "Right to reply!" When I did, this polite, intellectual professor screamed from across the room, "No! He has been given enough time already!"

Their intention had been to come and neatly seduce us all, but now their plans had come to nothing.

I did not stand up and say, "Thus says the Lord," but said only, "I'd like to read a scripture." This scripture acted as a spear, a sword and a lance that caused total chaos. The professor completely lost his head and several others turned to me and shouted, "How lacking in love!"

They tried to interrupt the whole discussion. I wondered to myself, "What should I do now?" They had virtually begun to jump on top of me.

Then I sensed the Lord telling me, "Go forward and shake hands with one of the homosexuals and tell him that I love him."

So I went up, extended my hand and said, "Jesus loves you!"

"I'm not touching your hand," he said. "If I had my way, I would spit in your face."

"That wouldn't matter," I said. "You can do that if you like, but you need to know that Jesus loves you anyway. He loves you and He has a wonderful plan for your life."

I just stood there, speaking the love and freedom of God to him: "You can be set free. You can be released from this bondage." As I said these things, I could feel my knees shaking. There was such a confrontation in the spirit world.

If you were to examine this whole situation on a superficial level, you might feel, "How terrible! Things were really stirred up. It couldn't have been God since people got so disturbed." Yet God is present even in the middle of disturbances. The following semester they did not dare to hold a public discussion. Instead, the students were divided into smaller groups. But even then there were people in each of the small groups who stood up for the Word of God.

Treachery on Every Level

This treachery is taking place today in schools, companies and within political debates, not just regarding homosexuality, but also concerning the New Age movement and occultism. Wherever you look you will discover this "sophisticated" form of seduction. Some Christians have even become so sophisticated that they too have swallowed these things. It is time that we stood up and kicked the devil out of every single area where he has found an entrance.

There is no reason why we should have to follow the devil's rules. God plays according to different rules. Even if the devil presents himself politely, intellectually and seductively, you can prophesy in the broadest dialect and say, "Thus says the Lord!" God looks at the heart! He is looking for prophets who will prophesy in the Holy Spirit—not for people who just run around getting angry at others or who have no more than personal opinions to shout about everything.

In the story I related, you can see how clever the devil's strategy is. By influencing future priests he tries to get his message to people all over the country. This is also why the devil is so angry at us. If we are able to gather over 800 Bible school students, hundreds of preachers and several thousand believers from all over the world, we have the ability to shake nations!

We do not preach just to get a general hallelujah-reaction, but in order to see results. God wants to see results and He wants to see circumstances changed. We desire to influence people, not in a natural, human manner, but in the Holy Spirit.

We refuse to accept this country as it is right now. We refuse to watch our nation perish. We refuse to accept a backslidden Body of Christ. We refuse to accept whitewashed walls. Neither can we accept a presentation of the Gospel that is cute or pleasant. The Gospel must be presented as it really is. We will not accept anything but the glory and the power of God.

Entire nations can turn to God. Therefore, the message is the same today as it was in the days of Jeremiah: *Land, hear the word of the Lord!*

24

Woes From Heaven

O Lord, You induced me, and I was persuaded; You are stronger than I, and have prevailed. I am in derision daily; Everyone mocks me. For when I spoke, I cried out; I shouted, "Violence and plunder!" Because the word of the Lord was made to me a reproach and a derision daily (Jer 20:7-8).

This country needs people who will complain, although not as the world complains or as many Christians do when they grumble about their taxes. We need people who complain in God and bring woes from heaven.

Just as Jesus pronounced woes on the Pharisees and Jeremiah shouted violence and plunder, we need to hear what God has to say about the violence in our countries. For instance, the Holy Spirit has something to say about the fact that 15 year-olds have their throats cut on the streets of our capital city, as was the case recently here in Sweden.

People sit on television debate programs and try to solve these problems, endlessly talking and sharing their opinions. Eventually, they stand helpless to do anything. They are spiritually blind and so they grope about in the dark. God, however, has a solution to these problems.

Violence—A Result of Ungodliness

What is the real reason behind the current situation? What has happened to our country?

Behold, the day! Behold, it has come! Doom has gone out; the rod has blossomed, pride has budded. Violence has risen up into a rod of wickedness (Ezek 7:10-11).

Key positions in our countries have been given over to ungodliness and, as a result, it has spread throughout the land. Violence has risen up as a rod of wickedness. Only those who have the Lord as their security can provide protection and security for the people of our country.

If the citizens confess that the Lord is our fortress, our rock, our stronghold, our sun, our shield and our Father, and if we hide in the shadow of the Almighty, we can halt the problem of violence in our nation. But when ungodly men and women believe that they can do this themselves, God will show them that violence actually rises up as a rod of wickedness.

Deliver me from my enemies, O my God; defend me from those who rise up against me. Deliver me from the workers of iniquity, and save me from bloodthirsty men. For look, they lie in wait for my life; the mighty gather against me, not for my transgression nor for my sin, O Lord. They run and prepare themselves through no fault of mine. Awake to help me, and behold! You therefore, O Lord God of hosts, the God of Israel, awake to punish all the nations; Do not be merciful to any wicked transgressors.... At evening they return, They growl like a dog, And go all around the city. Indeed, they belch out with their mouth; swords are in their lips; for they say, "Who hears?" But You, O Lord, shall laugh at them; you shall have all the nations in derision. O You his Strength, I will wait for You. For God is my defence; my merciful God shall come to meet me; God shall let me see my desire on my enemies. Do not slay them, lest my people forget; scatter them by Your power, and bring them down, O Lord our shield. For the sin of their mouth and the words of their lips, let them even be taken in their pride, and for the cursing and lying which they speak. Consume them in wrath, consume them, that they may not be; and let them know that God rules in Jacob to the ends of the earth.... And at evening they return, they growl like a dog, and go all around the city. They wander up and down for food, and howl if they are not satisfied. But I will sing of Your power; Yes, I will sing aloud of Your mercy in the morning; for You have been my defence and refuge in the day of my trouble. To You, O my Strength, I will sing praises; for God is my defence, the God of my mercy (Ps 59:1-17).

God has complete protection for those who love Him, even in the midst of a violent generation.

In the light of the New Covenant, Psalm 59, which we read above, is not about people, but about the demons that drive people to wander restlessly in search of blood, to attack people randomly and engage in unprovoked violence.

In the Holy Spirit, we can pray for a total change. There is no reason why we should tolerate violence on our streets. We can stand against it in the Name of Jesus, pray against it and expect the Word of God to find an entrance into these people's hearts.

The Glory of God on the Streets

There are countless young people just waiting to be saved. There is no reason why home videos full of violence should influence them to commit murder or many other things they had never previously imagined doing, not even in their wildest dreams.

They do these things because demons force them out on the streets to wander aimlessly. They stay out all night and lie in ambush for innocent people on their way home. These young people need to receive Jesus as their Lord and Savior so that the glory of God fills the streets instead.

God will be able to do this when we pray for it, prophesy against violence and reveal the real cause behind it. The reason behind increased violence is not the lack of policemen, although there are indeed too few police.

Neither is the violence due to poor legislation, although such legislation does exist. More than anything else, the real reason behind violence is ungodliness. However, God can change the situation so that people begin to seek Him instead.

For when I spoke, I cried out; I shouted, "Violence and plunder!" Because the word of the Lord was made to me a reproach and a derision daily. Then I said, "I will not make mention of Him, Nor speak anymore in His name." But His word was in my heart like a burning fire shut up in my bones; I was weary of holding it back, and I could not (Jer 20:8-9).

The fire on Jeremiah's lips was shut up in his bones and this began to make him feel miserable. No one feels worse or more frustrated than a disobedient prophet, who refuses to speak on the Lord's behalf. When Jeremiah finally made up his mind and said, "I must say only what God says, no matter the cost," his anointing returned.

The Spirit of God and the strength of God came upon him and he became once again what he was intended to be. This resulted in great changes in the circumstances surrounding him.

The most dangerous thing we can do when God has spoken to us is to allow others to hold us back or persuade us to keep quiet or compromise. This shuts the message of God up inside us and causes us frustration and difficulty. Not only this, but the words that were intended to go out and help set others free, remain unspoken.

As a result, people wander around homeless and backslidden. They fail to meet Jesus in the way they should. Their lives never produce any real, lasting fruit nor do they attain the heights of revelation that they ought to reach.

What is supposed to be the glorious Bride of Christ becomes a gray, religious, backslidden mass. However, no one can change this distressing situation quite like the prophet who refuses to shut up the word of the Lord but instead releases it. This word will come forth like a hammer and bring order to the people of God so that we do what we are called to do: change nations in the power of the Holy Spirit.

THE PROPHETIC WORD

25

Two Kinds of Prophecy

And in these days prophets came from Jerusalem to Antioch. Then one of them, named Agabus, stood up and showed by the Spirit that there was going to be a great famine throughout all the world, which also happened in the days of Claudius Caesar. Then the disciples, each according to his ability, determined to send relief to the brethren dwelling in Judea. This they also did, and sent it to the elders by the hands of Barnabas and Saul (Acts 11:27-30).

There are two different kinds of prophecy and Agabus operated in both of them. Here in Acts 11, he brings a general prophecy. It is not directed toward a specific individual, but it is a general word of prophecy that applies to the social, physical, geographical and political events in the world and their subsequent relation to the Church.

General Prophecy

In this instance, the prophecy was about a famine, or a social change, which would affect the Church negatively. Therefore, the Spirit of God wished to inform the Church of this future event so it could prepare for this time and come through it in victory. The prophecy was a general prophetic message regarding events to come on a worldwide scale. It was given in relation to the Church, allowing the Church to protect and prepare itself and retain the initiative in what it has been called to do.

185

When such a message is given, it is important to respond as the Christians in Acts did. They took the prophecy seriously and immediately began to make the necessary preparations.

Sadly though, there have been many prophecies that have been treated merely as a little decoration in the middle of a meeting. Afterwards when people are asked what they thought about the message of prophecy, it is clear that although they may be enthusiastic about it, they have not really held it in their hearts, and cannot remember what it was about.

Prophecy is not intended to be a decoration for a meeting; it is a word from God. Therefore you should pay attention to prophecies, write them down and meditate on them so that they enter your spirit. If they come from God, then heaven is speaking to you. Their purpose is often for you to pray, and therefore it is vital that you act in accordance with the prophetic word.

As already mentioned, the rebuilding of the temple after the Babylonian captivity did not meet with such success because of the amount of cement or the strong men who carried sand and stone, but because of the prophets who were constantly engaged in prophesying. We read that through the prophets, the temple was built successfully. The same principle applies in the New Covenant.

General prophecy is on a high level and is directed to the whole world. This is the first type of prophecy.

Personal Prophecy

The second kind of prophecy is a personal prophecy, such as when a prophet of the Lord goes to another of the Lord's servants or to a brother or sister and prophesies about something concerning that person's personal life. This may apply to his or her relationship with God or to their future.

An example of this type of prophecy is found in Acts 21 *, 10* when the prophet Agabus came down from Judea and prophesied over Paul. He took Paul's belt, wrapped it around himself and said, "This is what will happen to this man."

The other brothers who were there did not want Paul to die and were therefore distressed. But Paul knew the prophecy did not mean that he was going to die, but that it was intended to prepare him for what would happen in Jerusalem. He knew that when he arrived in the city there would be tumultuous times of great difficulty, but he also knew what God had said; that he would not die in Jerusalem.

Paul was willing to die for Jesus at any time because he had already given his whole life to Him. He was on his way to Jerusalem, but not in order to die; he knew that God had said he would also preach in Rome. So he received the prophecy in the spirit in which it was intended and was prepared for what lay ahead.

We see then these two different ways in which the prophet operates with the prophetic message. There are many examples of general prophecy in the Old Testament. The Lord told Jeremiah to prophesy over Edom, Babylon and many other places. On the other hand, personal prophecies, with a supernatural anointing are also given directly into people's situations. Both are supernatural and both forms of prophecy contain divine revelation.

26

Messages from God

While on his third missionary journey, Paul once stayed at the home of Philip who had previously been a deacon but who was now in the ministry of an evangelist.

Now this man had four virgin daughters who prophesied. And as we stayed many day, a certain prophet named Agabus came down from Judea. When he had come to us, he took Paul's belt, bound his own hands and feet, and said, "Thus says the Holy Spirit, 'So shall the Jews at Jerusalem bind the man who owns this belt, and deliver him into the hands of the Gentiles.' " And when we heard these things, both we and those from that place pleaded with him not to go up to Jerusalem. Then Paul answered, "What do you mean by weeping and breaking my heart? For I am ready not only to be bound, but also to die at Jerusalem for the name of the Lord Jesus." So when he would not be persuaded, we ceased, saying, "The will of the Lord be done" (Acts 21:9-14).

The prophet reveals the will of the Lord. Agabus took Paul's belt, wrapped it around himself and began to prophesy. He carried out a prophetic deed. The Bible is full of this kind of prophetic action. They cannot be invented, but they are inspired by the Holy Spirit at a specific moment.

In this instance, Agabus took Paul's belt and told him what would happen to him. Immediately the others reacted against the will of God, and tried to persuade Paul to change his plans so these things would not happen. In certain places today, people would have undoubtedly escorted Agabus out because of his "negative" prophecy!

Paul, however, recognized the prophecy as the will of God. It was not the first time he had heard these words. He had heard the same thing several times before and this prophetic word acted as a confirmation. He already knew that he was meant to go to Jerusalem, and for this reason, the prophecy further confirmed this fact, which is exactly the purpose of prophecy.

The prophet's task is not only to bring a new word but also to confirm what God has already said.

Dare to Test Words of Prophecy

Do not purchase a ticket to some far away place just because someone prophesies over you that you are to go there, if you yourself do not sense a confirmation in your spirit that it is right.

At the same time, however, there are messages from God which will disturb your *mind* because you have never considered such things before, but your *spirit* will say, "This is right!" This kind of prophecy is correct. Even if someone prophesies over you that you will be a missionary in a place you have never heard of, it is possible for you to sense in your spirit that God is speaking to you. It is important for you to act on this kind of prophecy.

This is how the pentecostal revival in Brazil, possibly the biggest and most powerful pentecostal revival in the world, began. It started with two Swedes in South Bend, Indiana, down in the basement of a Baptist church that later became a Pentecostal church. They prayed and received a word from God that said, "Go to Pará!"

Since they had no idea where this was they asked, "Where is Pará?" They took out an atlas and found it in Brazil. An offering was taken, they were prayed for and separated for the ministry, and off they went.

In this way one of the mightiest Pentecostal revivals this world has ever seen began. It started with two men who went to a place which, to begin with, they could not even find on a map. When the Holy Spirit said the word, "Pará!" they realized that it was God speaking, found the place and went there.

God knows more than you and He can speak through words of prophecy. However, someone can say a lot of strange things and you may have no inner witness about them. Such prophecies often sound slightly religious and may put pressure on you, making you feel that "You have to do this."

There have been times when I have received a prophecy and said, "I don't even know if that is God. We'll see."

You may say, "But surely you can't be that disrespectful of prophecy, can you?"

However, this is not at all disrespectful. It is right to test words of prophecy. If it is done in the right spirit you can say, "God, if this is of you, I will gladly do it, but if it is not of you, then I don't want it. Show me whether or not it is of you."

God will always show you if it is from Him. You do not need to run off with some strange word you have been given. God is capable of saying the same thing again through different people to assure you that it is from Him. Without knowing about one another, different people can say exactly the same thing. Then you know that what you have heard is from heaven.

However, if you are unsure whether or not it is of God, do not let yourself be unnecessarily impressed, no matter what people do. Do not be distracted by a lot of sensationalism. There will be many distractions, particularly as we enter the nineties. Do not let them impress you. Ask God whether or not they are from heaven.

191

If a word is from God, it will have the ability to carry you throughout your life. If a prophet lies on his belly or stands on his hands to prophesy, it does not matter; as long as what he says is from God. But if you decide to believe him just because he stands on his hands, you have made a grave mistake.

27

The Attitude of Your Heart

Make up your mind to walk with God for the rest of your life. Even if this means that you have to change your "overcoat" once in a while, it will not harm you. When the old one wears out, all you have to do is to buy a new one. You need to decide that no matter what God is doing and no matter how He does it, by the grace of God, you will be a part of it.

It is possible for you to walk with God all of your life. You need to make this a vital part of your being, because you will be presented with many opportunities to back down and "take it easy" after you have been walking with Him for some time. Before you become fixed in your habits and behavior, you need to determine, not just once or twice but for as long as you are alive, to follow the Lord wherever He goes. This is the first major decision you need to make.

Nathanael—A Man Without Guile

Secondly, you must decide not to fight against anything you do not understand or comprehend. Instead, you can be like Nathanael, who was not sure whether or not Jesus was the Messiah (see John 1:45-51). He did not rise up against Him, but rather, he sat down beneath a fig tree and wondered what this Jesus was all about.

Perhaps he thought to himself, "There are so many prophet movements nowadays, and my brothers are so easily influenced. The slightest little thing that happens and they're a part of it. Now they're running after John the Baptist. Before that they were chasing someone else. That Philip just wants to be a part of everything."

"How am I supposed to know whether or not this is from God? And now Philip comes and tells me, 'We have met the Messiah.' The Messiah, for whom Israel has waited hundreds of years! And he says, 'We have met him!' "

"So where does he come from," Nathanael probably asked.

"From Nazareth!" would have come the answer.

"But Philip, the scriptures say nothing about Nazareth! He is supposed to come from Bethlehem. Don't you understand that? Is there anything else you'd like to tell me about him? Who is he, really?"

There is nothing wrong with wondering. There is nothing wrong with being cautious. *Discretion will preserve you,* it says in Proverbs 2:11, and this is one of the fruits of wisdom. It does not say that criticism, rebellion or carnal suspicion will preserve you; it says "discretion" will.

Nathanael knew that if Jesus really was the Messiah, then he would have to give Him his entire life. He would have to follow Him. There would be no room for doubt, and that is why he needed to know if Jesus was in fact the Messiah.

Figuratively speaking, he could not simply board a train and take the risk that, after a few miles, the conductor might say, "Unfortunately, no one is driving this train. It is moving all by itself," or "The engineer jumped off at the last station. He realized that he wasn't an engineer after all."

You cannot give your life to something that is so unsure. You can only really commit yourself to something that you know is secure and this is correct, since God has promised to show you the truth (John 16:13).

If anyone wants to do His will, he shall know concerning the doctrine, whether it is from God or whether I speak on My own authority (John 7:17).

You have the right to understand what you are getting into; and when you do understand it, you then must act on it. You have to commit yourself one hundred percent to it. Although things may fall apart on all sides and people around you react, provoke and attack, you know that what you have is from God. You must have a conviction about it.

Jesus did not say to Nathanael, "Nathanael, how dare you question my authority! Don't you know that I am the Messiah?" Instead, Jesus said, "Nathanael, I saw you beneath the fig tree."

"Oh, my goodness!" Nathanael must have exclaimed.

"Yes, I saw you there, and I see that there is no guile in you," Jesus continued.

God is looking among His servants and children today for people who are without guile. If there is guile in you, make sure you get rid of it!

Gamaliel's Principle

Acts 5:34-39 relates the story of Gamaliel addressing the Jewish council regarding what to do about the disciples. As he stood before them he said, "Let's wait and see what happens. Do not resist these men, because they might just be from God. And if you fight against them you will really be fighting against God Himself. On the other hand, if they are not from God then what they have will collapse. So whatever you do, don't resist them. Don't you remember that prophet who gathered 400 people but was killed and all of his followers were scattered? And we had another so-called prophet who drew many people away with him, he too was killed and his followers dispersed. If this is not from God it will fall, so you need not resist it.

However, if it is from God it will not fall, but you will. So don't fight against it." This was Gamaliel's advice.

Backslidden people, however, can never keep quiet. Bitterness cannot keep its mouth shut. Self-righteousness always has to criticize. However, even if you disagree with something or cannot understand it but remain in the spirit, you can keep quiet. You can weigh things in the spirit, carefully turning them over, and asking God, "Is this from you or not? What is this?"

However, those who are filled with carnality, rebellion, backsliding and lust for power are unable to keep quiet. They have to talk, have to act, have to criticize, have to attack. This is the nature of the spirit of Cain. It comes on people and forces them to do things they had never intended to do.

There is something that causes people who refuse to receive truth, to want to put a stop to it instead. If truth triumphs, it will shed light on these people, and others will see that there are things in their lives that really should not be there. Others will notice that they are not living as they ought to. This is why such people attempt to extinguish the truth before it begins to shine too brightly or comes too close.

"We need to do something about this," they say. "What should we do? I know, let's crucify Him. That sounds good."

The Truth is Always Resurrected

Poor Annas and Caiaphas! Three days after they had crucified Jesus, they were faced with a new problem which they had not counted on. They had never expected Him to rise from the dead. But truth is always resurrected.

Caiaphas stood mumbling and scratching his head and thinking to himself, "It will be nice to get rid of that Jesus. That's one less problem to solve. Now we can get back to keeping the peace between the Romans and the zealots and all the rest of them. We'll get things under control, I'm sure."

Three days later, however, Jesus was back on earth in His resurrection power, and, in Acts 4, it is obvious that things quickly went from bad to worse. Suddenly, there were Christians everywhere. They tried to throw them in prison, but they just came out again. They threw them in again, and once more they got out. The fact that Jesus was risen from the dead echoed throughout Jerusalem.

This is what Gamaliel knew—you cannot fight against the truth. Paul says, For we can do nothing against the truth, but for the truth (2 Cor 13:8).

Some people fall by the wayside. Demas, one of Paul's close disciples, fell after having been with Paul for several years. He undoubtedly could have said, "I was with Paul from the beginning. I know him intimately." However, this same man became very critical toward Paul and left him. Paul says of him, *Demas has forsaken me, having loved this present world* (2 Tim 4:10). Why did he forsake Paul? Because somewhere along the line the price was too much for him, somewhere in Demas' life there was guile.

The same was true of Judas. He followed Jesus for several years. He knew Him well, yet when it really mattered, he forsook Him.

"But Nathanael," said Jesus, "is a man without guile."

When Nathanael saw the truth, he was prepared to give his life to it. This did not require much revelation. He needed to receive some revelation, but not much, before he could see that Jesus was indeed the Messiah. When this conviction had entered his heart, nothing could cause him to go back on it. He became one of Jesus' disciples and later an apostle, and God used him during the rest of his earthly life.

This is how God wants to use you as well.

28

Give Heed to the Word!

Now I urge you, brethren, note those who cause divisions and offences, contrary to the doctrine which you learned, and avoid them. For those who are such do not serve our Lord Jesus Christ, but their own belly, and by smooth words and flattering speech deceive the hearts of the simple (Rom 16:17-18).

These two verses describe three different kinds of people. The first are the *simple people*. These are the children who will believe any stranger who comes and asks them if they would like some candy. In the same way, spiritual charlatans approach them and ask, "Would you like a few spiritual candies? Just follow me and everything will be fine." And the baby Christian, not knowing any better, does so.

The second category of Christian is the *one who deceives*. How do these people deceive others? Are they hard and loveless? Do they try to frighten people? Oh no! They are so very mild. They use smooth words and flattering speech! They are deceivers who come with nice, seductively packaged lies.

Hopefully you belong to the third category of Christians; *those who have pure hearts but who watch in the spirit*. They are innocent in their purity, without being naive or ignorant. They are not so loving that they have lost the ability to think, but they are good-hearted and pure, while also being watchful.

In the days to come, the gift of discerning of spirits will become more necessary than ever. We need to have the ability to discern people's motives so we can separate the sweet from the sour and the truth from lies, so that we will not be deceived by flattering speech.

Of course, we need to be generous and loving, but we must do what we have been called to do without letting someone's flattery jeopardize and destroy it. This is why our hearts must be innocent and why we must walk in purity. Our motives must be pure while we remain watchful in the spirit.

If you are mature in God, you will not let yourself be deceived by flattering speech. You have the ability to recognize when God is speaking. You know that He does not suddenly speak with a different voice.

When God speaks, a holy fear and purity result. His voice does not puff you up, flatter you or attract your ego. In fact, it actually puts your ego to death. God can speak with a tone other than just a mild one. His voice can sound like thunder on Zion.

Times of Speech—Times of Silence

When Peter wrote his second letter, he was an old man. There are a few liberal theologians who claim that he is not the author of this letter, but I am convinced that Peter is the one who wrote it. He knew that he had received a word of wisdom and a prophetic message regarding what would take place in the future.

Moreover I will be careful to ensure that you always have a reminder of these things after my decease. For we did not follow cunningly devised fables when we made known to you the power and coming of our Lord Jesus Christ, but were eyewitnesses of His majesty. For He received from God the Father honor and glory when such a voice came to Him from the Excellent Glory: "This is My beloved Son, in whom I am well pleased." And we heard this voice which came from heaven when we were with Him on the holy mountain (2 Pet 1:15-18).

There will be times when you too are on the holy mountain; times when you experience transformation glory and hear God speak. These are the most precious moments of your life. Such a powerful prophetic anointing is not a common occurrence. But God will give you more and more of it, since He desires to have a prophetic Church that constantly flows in a prophetic anointing.

You know that there have been unique times and moments in your life when God has spoken to you. The glory was there, the anointing was there, the angels were there, the Father was present and the Holy Spirit spoke to you. These were life-changing times as God's words went into your heart.

Noah experienced this. He was given a message from heaven: "Build an ark!" (Gen 6:14). He received no other message for a hundred years until the ark was finished. Then God told him, "Go into the ark!" God was pleased with Noah because he had accepted the prophetic word and worked for a hundred years on the basis of that one directive.

There is a time when the prophetic word comes to you, but there is also another time when prophetic words seem largely absent. Then, you must work and act on the word that God has already given to you. If you fail to do so, you will end up backsliding. Life will become empty and boring and you will sit there, longing for new revelations.

However, you are not meant to sit and long for new "flutterings" in the spirit world. Instead, you should be acting on the prophetic word you have already received.

There are times when God speaks and times when He does not. During the times when He does not speak, He expects you to act in accordance with His previous word to you. Perhaps to start with, when one prophecy after another was flooding over you, you may have felt impressed and thought that this would continue indefinitely.

But when the continuous flow of prophecy suddenly ceased, you wondered, "What has happened? Have I backslidden? What is this all about? Why aren't things quite as wonderful anymore?" The fact is that the word has already impregnated your spirit—it is now in your heart for you to act upon. This word is designed to carry you for the rest of your life.

Some people may receive only two or three prophecies during their entire lifetime, but this is enough to set their course and point them in the right direction for the rest of their lives. By this I do not mean that they receive a total of only two or three prophecies, but that there are certain prophetic messages that carry a greater strength and weight than others. They serve to define the direction of your life and ministry. These are the kinds of prophecies I am referring to.

We have already spoken about the prophet Agabus and seen how he spoke a prophecy into Paul's personal life that later helped him in a particular situation in Jerusalem. We have also seen how Agabus gave a general prophecy regarding a coming famine. This prophecy helped not only a particular individual, but the entire Body of Christ at that time to survive through a much larger event that affected the whole Roman empire. These prophetic messages brought encouragement, help and safety for those who paid attention and acted on them.

Words to the Church

Certain prophetic words are tremendously important. They have the capacity to rescue all of Christianity itself; if they are heard, that is. Other words go straight into your personal life and have the potential to carry you for the rest of your life if you take them seriously. Not many words are necessarily needed.

I have received prophetic words before—perhaps only three or four words—and bang! they went straight into my spirit. These same words sustained me through periods of darkness and confusion. This kind of word burns like a fire within you in every sort of circumstance. You cannot get away from what the Lord has said to you.

Therefore, you need to guard the words that God has spoken to you; not just the personal words, but also the prophetic messages that have been directed to your church. This is extremely important, whether the word comes directly to your pastor or to the church as a whole. The things God says to your pastor include you as well.

You have a responsibility to find out what God has spoken to your pastor and to the whole church. Find out what God has said regarding the area where you help in the church. Write down these prophecies. Keep them constantly before your eyes.

Your responsibility is to pray forth the things God has spoken and to make sure that what God has intended becomes a reality. Do not take the prophetic word lightly! Cherish it more than silver or gold. Preserve it, write it down, think it over, meditate on it and pray over it.

If you are a pastor and someone has prophesied over you in front of the church, you should not try to put it aside or be ashamed of it. Instead, you should stand up and say, "This is what the Lord has said, and I want you as a church to receive it. Then we will enter into it and see it become a reality in our church." You should also make sure that the messages that God has given to your church also reach your staff and become a part of their hearts.

And so we have the prophetic word made more sure, which you do well to heed as to a light that shines in a dark place, until the day dawns and the morning star rises in your hearts (2 Pet 1:19).

The prophetic word of God contains a sureness and stability. Always remember what God has said. What is not of God will fall. If you are an elderly person, return to your private journal or notes and remember the things that God said to you when you were young. You undoubtedly know what you have said to Him and what He has said to you. It is time to refresh your memory.

Some have shipwrecked their faith because they have not paid attention to the prophetic word. God had said fantastic things to them, but events did not turn out as they had imagined. What God had promised took a little longer than they had anticipated or was fulfilled in an unexpected way. They became disappointed with God, other people and themselves. They set aside the prophetic word and stepped backwards in retreat.

God Hears Your Promises

When our youngest son, Benjamin, was newly born, we asked a few ministers to bless him, one of whom was Sten Nilsson, my father-in-law. There was a powerful prophetic anointing present at this occasion. I remember in particular how one of the brothers had turned to Sten and prophesied. One of the things he said was, "You who has said, 'I want to go all the way with you.'"

In 1937, in Oskarshamn, the town in which Sten grew up, he had clearly said to God on a particular occasion, "I want to go all the way with you!" Then, almost 50 years later, a prophet, who knew nothing about this, came and said exactly those words; words from a particular time and place. God remembered what Sten had said during his childhood.

Let the Word Stand Firm

Beloved, I now write to you this second epistle (in both of which I stir up your pure minds by way of reminder), that you may be mindfully of the words which were spoken before by the holy prophets, and of the commandment of us, the apostles of the Lord and Savior, knowing this first: that scoffers will come in the last days, walking according to their own lusts, and saying, "Where is the promise of His coming? For since the fathers fell asleep, all things continue as they were from the beginning of creation" (2 Pet 3:1-4).

You should remember what has been prophesied, not only in the scriptures several thousand years ago, but also by God's holy prophets specifically to you.

The times we are now living in will be characterized not only by glory, but by mockery as well. These are not only times of joy, they are also times of scoffing.

Mockery and scoffing will rise up and spit in your face, saying, "Where is the promise of His coming? What has happened to all the prophecies? Where are the results? Did God really speak? Do you really believe that God has spoken to you? You were supposed to be such a great man of God and just look at you now! Here you are, a pitiful little office worker. You thought you were destined for greatness. What became of you?"

Do you know how you should respond when you hear the devil speak to you like this? You should say, "Things are going just great! I have the victory! Hallelujah!"

This is how you can respond when you have determined that the prophetic word will stand firm in your life. You have let the word become cemented into your spirit, given heed to it, meditated on it, looked at it and churned it over. You have examined it, prayed in tongues over it, thought about it, received it and rejoiced over it as a gift straight from heaven.

Do Not Treat
the Word of God With Contempt!

Your words were found, and I ate them, and Your word was to me the joy and rejoicing of my heart; for I am called by Your name, O Lord God of hosts (Jer 15:16).

I have chosen to pay attention to the prophetic word. I have a whole collection of prophetic messages that God has spoken to me at various times. I have prayed over them. At times I have forgotten them, but God has always reminded me of them again.

When I look at them I say, "Just think, this is what God has said!" Every time I do this I receive renewed strength. After a few years, I have seen things turn out exactly as God had said they would. Although I could hardly believe the message when it first came, it was eventually fulfilled.

Second Chronicles 20:20 says that those who believe in the prophets will prosper. Another translation says that they will be successful. Do not despise the word of God when it comes. Receive it and believe it, no matter how unusual it may sound. You know whether or not it is from God; you can judge this in your spirit.

Receive and obey this word and you will prosper and be successful. The Word of God will be fulfilled. You will be able to say, "The Lord has not failed to keep any of His promises. They were all completed." The scriptures say that the prophetic word is the most precious and valuable thing there is.

For both prophet and priest are profane; Yes, in My house I have found their wickedness," says the Lord. "Therefore thus says the Lord of hosts concerning the prophets: 'Behold, I will feed them with wormwood, and make them drink the water of gall; for from the prophets of Jerusalem Profaneness has gone out into all the land.' " For who has stood in the counsel of the Lord, and has perceived and heard His word? Who has marked His word and heard it? Behold, a whirlwind of the Lord has gone forth in fury—a violent whirlwind! It will fall violently on the head of the wicked. "I have not sent these prophets, yet they ran. I have not spoken to them, yet they prophesied. But if they had stood in My counsel, and had caused My people to hear My words, Then they would have turned them from their evil way and from the evil of their doings" (Jer 23:11, 15, 18-19, 21-22).

A true prophetic message is characterized by the fact that it always produces repentance, fear of God, purity and holiness. It never exalts self, nor does it create a false hope. It cuts away sin. It brings strong encouragement in God and always results in purity, with God in the center.

The Word is the Strongest Thing

"The prophet who has a dream, let him tell a dream; and he who has My word, let him speak My word faithfully. What is the chaff to the wheat?" says the Lord. "Is not My word like a fire?" says the Lord. "And like a hammer that breaks the rock in pieces?" (Jer 23:28-29)

We often assume that the most powerful things we can receive from God are visions, revelations, dreams and pictures. God does indeed reveal Himself to His prophets through pictures, in symbols and through dreams. Yet, sometimes there can be a surplus of such pictures as people soulishly imagine to have seen just about everything.

God does give people pictures, but we need to understand that a word from the Bible is much more precise. If you open your Bible and tell someone, "God gave me this verse to give to you," do not allow the devil to belittle this because it seems too simple, or just because others exalt themselves with all their fancy visions.

As the Bible says, "The prophet who has a dream, let him tell a dream; and he who has My word, let him speak My word faithfully. What is the chaff to the wheat?" In other words, dreams are fine, but compared to the Word of the Living God, they are like chaff to wheat.

The prophetic word from the scriptures, or from the Spirit of God in line with the scriptures, contains such a strength that you do not need to sweeten it with anything else. You do not need to add anything extra to it. It needs no embellishment or decoration. All you need is the Word straight from the throne of God.

Our facilities here at Word of Life Church were built on a single word. The Spirit of God came and said: "Build!" Everything we have today was built on the strength of that one word. Not even the devil himself, nor the principalities over Sweden, nor the little demons over Uppsala could hinder it. *"We also have the prophetic word made more sure, which you do well to heed."*

29

Prophetic Messages Full of Power

Don't let anyone look down on you because you are young, but set an example for the believers in speech, in life, in love, in faith and in purity. Until I come, devote yourself to the public reading of Scripture, to preaching and to teaching. Do not neglect your gift, which was given you through a prophetic message when the body of elders laid their hands on you. Be diligent in these matters; give yourself wholly to them, so that everyone may see your progress. Watch your life and doctrine closely. Persevere in them, because if you do, you will save both yourself and your hearers (1 Tim 4:12-16 NIV).

If you have received something through the laying on of hands or though prophecy, do not neglect it. Today, many people want the prophetic office, but rather than longing for something you do not have, start to cultivate what you do have. You should begin to thank God for what you have received, take care of it and do not neglect your gift. According to this passage, it came to you through prophecy.

The prophet transfers something new into your life.

Certain prophetic messages are more than just an encouragement from heaven; they are a transmission of anointing and power. When such a prophecy is delivered to you in the Holy Spirit, something is transferred; you get a gift from God. This does not apply just to the gifts of the Spirit. It simply means that either you received something that you did not have before, or that you gained new strength in something you already have.

The devil is aware of this and so the prophetic word of God makes him very angry.

A Word in Every Crisis

Whenever I have been in a crisis or faced with an important decision, I have always received a prophetic word from God that has carried me through these situations.

When a prophecy comes, it must first be judged. The Bible tells us to test prophecy. (Notice that it says test, not despise). It must be in agreement with the Word of God and not just a lot of nonsense. It must also harmonize with your inner witness. If you do not have an inner witness about a prophecy, you should not receive it.

"Yes, but I do not dare to reject it. It was such a fantastic preacher who prophesied over me," you may say.

But this does not matter. Even if an angel comes, you still have a right to test what he says. Of course if it really is from God, then you need to receive it. However, if you feel unsure about it, put it aside for a while, and say, "God, if this is really from you, then you can tell it to me again."

We cannot afford to take general scriptures—God's logos—and make them our rhema—God's specific word in a particular situation—unless this is what the Holy Spirit says.

The difference between the logos and the rhema Word of God is very important. You need to understand this otherwise you may begin to prophesy soulishly, based on what are only general biblical principles. However, prophecy is not a general principle from the Word of God, but a specific word in a particular situation to a certain individual or group of people. You need to know this difference.

God Said, "Bangladesh!"

EX

Let me give you an example from my personal life regarding how we should relate to prophecy that is from God.

During my time as a student chaplain in the city of Uppsala, I sometimes felt a longing to get away and travel. There was something in my spirit, although I was not quite sure what. I only knew that God had something else for me, but I did not know exactly what this was. Then one day I was given the opportunity to travel as a student worker and start a ministry among students in Dacca, Bangladesh. I felt a general longing to do this.

Soon afterwards, I was with several others in my office. One of them was Robert Ekh, who is now assistant pastor here at Word of Life, but at that time he was a Lutheran priest in Stockholm. Another brother, Klas Lindberg, who is currently one of the pastors of Södermalms Church in Stockholm, was also present. A powerful word of prophecy came for me through Klas. There was no question that this message was straight from heaven. It was more than just a prophecy—the whole room was filled with the glory of God. It was wonderful.

The message said that God would take me to Bangladesh and that many things would happen, not just among students, but among women and children in particular. Several concrete directives came in this message.

When we left that place I was convinced. There was no doubt about it; I was going to be a student chaplain in Bangladesh. It was obviously from God. We all heard Him say it! I accepted the calling, and my family and I began to make preparations to leave. However, we gradually began to notice that we were lacking any inner joy or excitement.

We got hold of books about Bangladesh in order to read them, but I never read them properly. I only skimmed through them. They were full of statistics about how bad the situation was, and I could not seem to bring myself to read them.

My wife, Birgitta, was born and raised in India. We talked about how nice it would be among the palms and mangoes as we spoke about what we would do there. We finally came to the conclusion that we would sit on the roof at dusk and eat mangoes. We thought to ourselves, "What is going on?"

After a few months had gone by, we still had not talked everything through properly with one another. Other people had already begun to introduce us as missionaries. Letters were circulated that contained our picture and we were about to be introduced to the missionary organization. We attended a missions conference and everyone looked at us and thought, "They're going to Bangladesh."

"What do we do now?" I thought. It all began to feel very strange, and I began to wonder what we had got ourselves into.

The contract included an education and salary. Our traveling expenses were to be covered. When we got there we would have servants, a house and the possibility of some sort of vehicle as well. Everything was packaged and ready to go. All I needed to do was step into it. But as time went on, it felt increasingly wrong.

The confusing thing was the prophecy that my dear brother had brought. I knew beyond a doubt that it had come from God. However, the situation grew worse with every passing day.

God Said, "Tulsa!"

After three months of this, we discovered that we could do something very interesting: we could pray and really ask God about it! It took us a whole three months to figure this out. So we got down on our knees and prayed and as clear as crystal we heard God say, "You are not to go to Bangladesh, you are to go to Tulsa, Oklahoma."

"Oh, no!" I thought to myself, "from the world's poorest country to the world's richest!"

I could just see the missions committee in front of me as I said, "Well, I've been praying and fasting and the Lord has told me not to go to the mission field, but to go to America instead!" I could just hear their reaction. Nonetheless, this is indeed what God had said, in spite of the fact that I did not understand it.

"What about the prophecy?" I asked Him.
The Spirit of God responded, "Just let it rest. Pay no attention to it."

I thought to myself, "Was it a false prophecy? If it was, then I am a schizophrenic, God does not exist and the anointing is nothing but excitement." I had difficulty understanding the situation.

But I put aside the prophecy and began making arrangements to visit Tulsa. Suddenly, the situation had turned around completely. When we had planned to go to Bangladesh, everything was paid and prearranged. But when I wrote to Rhema Bible Training Center in Tulsa and applied to their Bible school, I received a negative reply. They were unable to admit foreign students.

I went to the American embassy to apply for a visa. Getting a visa proved to be no problem—as long as I could show a letter of acceptance from the Bible school!

I said, "No, I haven't been accepted at the school yet."

"Well, as soon as you receive a letter of acceptance from the school, we will give you a visa. The school you plan to attend must be registered with the authorities. If it is, you will easily get a proof of acceptance and then you will have your visa and everything will be settled!" said the embassy.

So I wrote a letter to the Bible school and explained to them that I needed a letter of acceptance in order to get a visa. "Yes," they said, "but we are not registered with the authorities."

"You're not?" I asked. "Then how am I supposed to get a visa?"

I returned to the embassy and tried again, but to no avail. When I turned to the school, the answer was no; when I turned to the embassy, it was also no. Only when I turned to God was the answer yes.

Then we had to deal with the missions committee. At first, they were unwilling to let me go. On top of that, they wanted to know how I would be able to afford it. I had no money, no visa and no letter of acceptance from the school—I had nothing at all.

In the first case, everything was arranged and ready; in the second case nothing was fixed at all. All I had to go on was a word from heaven, another word which pointed in a totally different direction. It was enough to make a person extremely confused.

However, what God had said grew stronger and stronger and faith began to come. This faith also began to grow: "In the Name of Jesus, we are going to Tulsa. I know that God has said it, and we are going to get there." We stood in faith. There were many events that took place to finally bring us to the Bible school in Tulsa, but we did get there, and we attended for one year.

The Word is Fulfilled

Just before we were due to leave, in August 1981, we held a pastors' conference. This was the first such conference in Sweden that offered faith teaching, and it proved to be the start of the annual faith conference that we have held every year since then. The conference was two weeks long and was attended by 20 pastors each week. Sam Whaley and Jim Kaseman came from the United States to teach us.

During this conference I was approached by Bengt Sundberg (who is currently Missions Director here at Word of Life Church) who asked me, "How would you like to visit Bangladesh sometime?"

"Yeah, sure, "I said, and imagined taking such a trip in five or ten years. At the same time, however, something was bursting within me and I heard the Holy Spirit say, "This is what I was talking about." Then I put it out of my mind completely.

We left for the States and were there for one year. When we later returned, I began to travel and preach in Sweden. Before long, Bengt Sundberg approached me again and asked if I wanted to go right away.

So we went to Bangladesh and had a powerful week there. God healed women and children in particular. It was marvelous for me to see how everything God had said was fulfilled, right down to the smallest detail.

I had no idea at first how it would come to pass. I had tried to organize things myself, but it turned out to be the wrong channel, the wrong way and the wrong time— although there was nothing wrong with the prophecy itself. When I had calmed down and put it to one side, God knew exactly how to bring it to pass. In the fullness of time it became manifest, and it turned out exactly as God had said it would.

Dare to Reconsider the Word!

Perhaps you have received a word of prophecy but have formed a preconception of how it will be fulfilled. If this is your situation, then I would urge you to lay the whole thing down. If it seems difficult and causes you confusion, then do not be afraid to reconsider the prophecy.

Do not create a lot of selfish ambitions. Never try to decide *how* a prophecy should be fulfilled. Decide only *that* it will be fulfilled; if it is from God, that is.

If you know that it is from God, then you can stop wondering about how or when it will take place. These things are not your concern. *Though it tarries, wait for it; Because it will surely come, It will not tarry* (Hab 2:3). Be like Mary, who considered what God said and treasured it in her heart. In the fullness of time, it will come to pass. God will do what He has promised in your life.

Do not become frustrated if what has been prophesied does not happen immediately. Find out first if it contains a condition. If the Lord says, "If you do this, then I will do this," then there is something you must do first. So find out what the conditions are.

Secondly, you need to consider the aspect of time. If you fail to realize that prophetic timing is not the same as our timing, you will have problems. God's time perspective is different to ours. To us, "soon" means tomorrow. But it has been 2,000 years since the Lord said that He was coming soon. This "soon" has obviously not yet come.

Just because God says something, does not mean that it will be fulfilled tomorrow. If the Lord says, "Go to Africa!" this does not mean that you should leave the next day. It may actually take 10-15 years for certain prophecies to come to pass.

Just because it may take time to happen it does not mean that God has forgotten what He has said. He has a purpose. For example, God has a special time schedule for the return of Jesus and there is a reason for this; He desires that the whole world be saved. He lets the return of Jesus wait until precisely the right moment, so that as many as possible will be saved and come to heaven (2 Pet 3:9).

God does not forget the words He has spoken to you, but it may take a long time before they are manifested. In the meantime, keep the Word in your heart and let it shine like a light in the darkness. You can know and be confident during the whole time that God means what He has said.

The Words Went into My Spirit

The type of prophetic message like the one I have just described is extremely significant. I remember in 1980, when I traveled with a good friend and visited various ministers in America. We were asked out to eat at a restaurant by a couple whom we had just met. As we were sitting eating, the woman suddenly turned to her husband, and asked, "Albert, may I prophesy?" He looked at her and said, "Yes, you may."

Then she began to prophesy over me by saying, "You will stand and preach in front of thousands of people! And you will teach many pastors. You will preach to pastors." She continued speaking, and what she said became all the more fantastic.

Then she said something else: "But you will be able to do it only because you will never forget your background. You know where I took you from. You know how you were before you knew me. Because you will always be mindful of the pit from which I took you, I will always be able to keep you humble by pointing to where you came from. In this way I will continue to be able to use you."

I did not have a pen and paper. I did not have a tape recorder. But I certainly remember these words. They went directly into my spirit. I had no idea how they would be fulfilled, but something happened in my life at that moment. Something was given to me. And it has been there ever since, not just as an encouragement from heaven, but as something that is real and concrete.

A Word for the Bible School

In the summer of 1982 we held a pastors' conference in Jönköping, Sweden. At one point during the conference there was a prophecy that came for me regarding the fact that God wanted me to start a Bible school. He said, "I have asked others to do it, but they have not wanted to. Now I am asking you to do it, and now you must do it."

God had spoken to me about the same thing previously, and I had planned to do it, although at some point in the future. Through this message I felt God was saying, "You must begin now—immediately!" So the Bible school started in the power of this prophecy. We set to work right away and were able to begin in the fall of 1983.

A Word About the Church

When we started Word of Life Church, a message came which said, "This church will grow slowly. It will grow gradually, one step at a time. Eventually it will become bigger and bigger. It will take time, and it will happen slowly. But step by step it will grow and will be a large church."

My immediate reaction was, "That's too bad!" I wanted the church to explode. It is easy to have a lot of your own private dreams and ideas.

Now, seven years later, I can state that our growth has taken place exactly in line with this word. It took a long time for us to grow to a membership of 500; approximately five years. Since then, it has begun to gain speed. Today, in April 1990, we have over 1,200 members in the congregation and many others who regularly attend our meetings; and we are getting bigger every month. In retrospect I can see how important it was for the church to grow at this pace. God was able to implant the needed stability and strength, especially with regard to the Bible school.

A New Direction

I carried this prophecy about the church with me until 1987. That year Ray McCauley, from Rhema in South

Africa, was one of the visiting speakers at our faith conference and the inauguration of our new facilities. He prophesied and said, "God has raised you up, not just to have the Bible school and not only to serve other men of God and other churches. God will lead you in an entirely new direction, to build a church that will speak to the entire nation. And just as my people have come this week, you will have this many people on Sundays. Then it will increase and the balcony will also be filled. People will come from all over Europe to see what God is doing here. God is going to change some of the things that you are doing. God has said this because several of those who work here and are members in the church need to know it."

God is able to lead us one step at a time. You can urge people on by shouting, "We want 10,000 members in 1990 and 15,000 by 1992." Then when these dates come, you end up looking a fool. Let God take you one step at a time instead. If it is from Him, the word will be fulfilled, as long as we are willing to change and adjust those things that relate to the prophetic message.

On the strength of that word we built a balcony last summer, in 1989. We did not build it just to be used for conferences. It cost us seven million Swedish kronor. I was almost angry when I heard the first estimate and I asked God, "Are we really supposed to pay so much money just so people can come and sit here one week out of the year?" This was my first response. Why should Word of Life Church have to shell out such a huge sum of money just so people can come here and enjoy themselves for one week?

But God spoke to me and said, "You don't need this just for the conference. It will be used for much more than just one conference. But you need to do it now. If you don't, it will cost you several million more in the future. So just swallow it. I will take care of it. You need the balcony."

As soon as we had finished building it, God began to speak. He began to tell us the many things for which the balcony would be used. Suddenly I began to understand. I had not had faith for these things, but at that point I began to receive it.

The Word Carries You Through

A few years ago as I drove past the empty field where Word of Life Church now stands, the Lord spoke to me. He said that five thousand people would attend our church services. I just about slammed on the brakes and drove the car off the road.

I was unable to receive this. Just the thought of it filled me with unbelief! We were in the process of building at that point and I could hardly bear the thought. Rather than receive the word mentally, I wanted to have it as a revelation in my spirit. As a result, I refused to receive it at all.

One year passed, and God admonished me sternly because I still had not received what He had told me. Then He said, "Let me help you. Count how many people there are at a Sunday morning meeting, the children included."

"Over two thousand," I said.

"So having five thousand in attendance isn't so strange after all, is it?"

"No, I guess not," I replied, and I felt faith for this enter my heart. The first time the word came I did not have any faith for it, but at that point I did. I could feel faith begin to sprout. I knew it would come to pass.

There will come a day when you will look back over your life and realize that every prophetic word was fulfilled. In the meantime, you will receive great strength if you receive what God says, allow it to enter your heart and thank the Lord for it. The Word will carry you through.

The Word of God is true. He is eager to see it fulfilled. He is longing to communicate with you. His care for you is so great that He desires to share His plans with you. He longs to guide you in paths of righteousness.

For this reason He is eager to reveal His word to you. When you listen, receive and hold fast to the word, you will witness the plan of God being fulfilled in your life and, like Joshua, you too will eventually be able to say, *Not a word failed of any good thing which the Lord had spoken to the house of Israel. All came to pass* (Josh 21:45).

Books by Ulf Ekman

A Life of Victory
The guidance, help and inspiration you need to put God's Word first. Fifty-four chapters, each dealing with a particular area of the believer's life. *288 pages.*

The Apostolic Ministry
How do we recognise an Apostle? What role does the Apostle have? What can we learn from the life of Paul, the greatest Apostle? Ulf Ekman gives Biblical guidance in this book. *128 pages.*

The Authority in the Name of Jesus
When you receive a revelation of what the name of Jesus really means, you will have boldness like never before. *Booklet, 32 pages.*

The Church of the Living God
The Church of the Living God is something far beyond what we think or experience. It is the place where the End-time Revival will have its source and climax—and you have a place in that Church. *158 pages.*

Destined for Victory
God has victorious plans for you. His plans never fail! In this book you will discover: • How to aviod fear of failure • How to withstand the attacks of Satan • How spiritual laws operate and • How Gods Word always brings results. *Booklet, 32 pages.*

Destroy the Works of the Devil
Jesus came to earth to destroy the works of the devil. His death on the cross struck Satan a death blow. Jesus triumphed over him and won the victory for YOU! *Booklet, 32 pages.*

Doctrine—The Foundations of the Christian Faith
Ulf Ekman gives an objective and biblical account of each fundamental doctrine of the Christian faith. In days when the Christian message is increasingly diluted and twisted *Doctrine* will be an asset for every pastor, leader and believer. *256 pages.*

Faith that Overcomes the World
Explains how faith arises, how it becomes operational, and what makes it grow. *140 pages.*

Financial Freedom
A thorough, biblical study on money, riches and material possessions. *128 pages.*

God is a Good God
God has given you abundantly more than you can ever grasp for your entire lifetime. This book examines God's character and nature, and reveals His overflowing love for you. *Booklet, 32 pages.*

God, the State and the Individual
God not only deals with individuals, but with nations and governments. You can change the destiny of your nation! *112 pages.*

God Wants to Heal Everyone
Discover the wonderful fact that God's will is to heal everyone—including you. *Booklet, 32 pages.*

The Holy Spirit
The Holy Spirit is your guide, your teacher, your counselor and your helper. Discover how you can live each day in the power of the Holy Spirit. *Booklet, 32 pages.*

I Found my Destiny
Follow Ulf Ekman from his boyhood home in Gothenburg to "Livets Ord" – Word of Life Church in Uppsala, Sweden. From 1983 until today Word of Life has become a center for education, evangelism, mission and reformation in Sweden and throughout the world. *150 pages.*

Jesus Died for You
Blessing is a daily reality when you understand the power of the cross:
• Satan's plans were crushed • Sickness was defeated • Poverty was broken
• Depression turned to joy. *Booklet, 32 pages.*

The Jews—People of the Future
Clarifies basic truths about the people and the land. Historical facts and biblical prophecies combine to reveal the fulfillment of God's End-time Plan. *160 pages.*

The Lord is a Warrior
You need to know who your enemy is, what your position of victory is and how to take up arms against that enemy. A handbook in spiritual warfare. *140 pages.*

The Power in the New Creation
A new dimension of victorious living awaits you. The Lord is with you, Mighty Warrior! *Booklet, 32 pages.*

Prayer Changes Nations
Ulf Ekman teaches here on what characterizes the time before revival, the work that needs to be done and how the Holy Spirit can change every believer into a bold prayer-warrior. *156 pages.*

The Prophetic Ministry
"Provides essential guideposts for the operation of the prophetic ministry today." From the Foreword by Demos Shakarian. *210 pages.*

Available from your local Christian bookstore, or order direct from the publisher.